GENDER AND ECONOMICS

Most economists now agree that economic theories have given little attention to subjects that are important for women, such as the position of women in the labour market, and the economic value of household and caring tasks. *Gender and Economics: A European Perspective* redresses this imbalance with this introduction to gender studies in economics. Areas discussed include:

- The important theories – from New Home Economics to the neo-institutionalist approach.
- The European perspective including a chapter on Central and Eastern Europe.
- Regular and atypical forms of employment and their consequences for gender distribution of job-holding and income.
- European Union policies, in particular affirmative action and comparable worth.

This is the first book in gender economics to address the institution and peculiarities of the European labour market, which are radically different from those of the United States. *Gender and Economics* uniquely combines practice and policy matters with theoretical issues, making it particularly useful to students and professionals.

Anneke Geske Dijkstra is Senior Lecturer in the Economics of Development at the Institute of Social Studies, The Hague.

Janneke Plantenga is Lecturer at the Economic Institute at the University of Utrecht. She is the Dutch member of the European network of experts on the situation on women in the labour market.

GENDER AND ECONOMICS

A European Perspective

Edited by A. Geske Dijkstra and Janneke Plantenga

London and New York

First published 1997
by Routledge
11 New Fetter Lane, London EC4P 4EE

Simultaneously published in the USA and Canada
by Routledge
29 West 35th Street, New York, NY 10001

© 1997 A. Geske Dijkstra and Janneke Plantenga

Typeset in Garamond by LaserScript, Mitcham, Surrey
Printed and bound in Great Britain by
Creative Print and Design (Wales), Ebbw Vale

British Library Cataloguing in Publication Data
A catalogue record for this book is available from the British Library

Library of Congress Cataloging in Publication Data
Gender and economics: a European perspective/edited by
A. Geske Dijkstra and Janneke Plantenga.
p. cm.
Includes bibliographical references and index.
1. Women – Europe – Economic conditions.
2. Women – Employment – Europe.
3. Discrimination in employment – Government policy – Europe.
I. Dijkstra, A. Geske. II. Plantenga, Janneke, 1956– .
HQ1587.G44   1997
331.4′094 – dc20   96-41437
CIP

ISBN 0–415–15424–3
ISBN 0–415–15425–1 (pbk)

CONTENTS

FIGURES AND TABLES

FIGURES

TABLES

vii

CONTRIBUTORS

Jeanne de Bruijn studied Sociology of Work at the University of Groningen, did her Ph.D. at the University of Wageningen and is now Professor in Gender Studies at the Free University of Amsterdam and responsible for the research group Policy, Culture and Gender Issues. She is a member of the Netherlands Research School of Women's Studies and has published on the history of women's work, sexual harassment, gender and care policy and comparable worth and equal pay. She was co-editor of *Women's Movement: History and Theory* (with Loes Derksen), 1993, Aldershot (Avebury); of *Gender and Organizations – Changing Perspectives* (with Eva Cyba), 1994, Amsterdam (Free University Press); and of *Inzichten in Vrouwenstudies: Uitdagingen voor beleidsmakers* ('Women's studies perspectives: challenges for policymakers'), 1995, The Hague (VUGA).

Anneke Geske Dijkstra studied Sociology and Economics at the University of Groningen, and obtained her Ph.D. in Economics from the same University. She is now senior lecturer in Economics of Development at the Institute of Social Studies in The Hague. She held previous positions at the Universities of Leiden, Groningen and Limburg, at the Open University and at the Institute for Economic Research of the University of El Salvador. Her main fields of interest include trade and industrialization policies and gender issues in relation to the performance of the macro-economy. She published *Industrialization in Sandinista Nicaragua – Policy and Practice in a Mixed Economy*, 1992, Boulder, Col. (Westview).

Anneke van Doorne-Huiskes studied Sociology at the University of Utrecht and has a Ph.D. in Sociology from the same University. Since 1991 she has been a Professor of Women's Studies at the Faculty of Social Sciences of the Erasmus University of Rotterdam. Past working affiliations include the Universities of Utrecht and Wageningen. She also works as a consultant for organizational change and equal opportunities policy. She has published books and articles on women's and men's careers, pay differences between men and women, comparable worth, and the effects of equal opportunities policies. In 1995, she edited *Women and the*

European Labour Markets (with J. van Hoof and E. Roelofs), London (Paul Chapman).

Siv Gustafsson is Professor of Economics (Comparative Population and Gender Economics) at the University of Amsterdam (1989–). She has a Ph.D. from Stockholm School of Economics (1976). She was a research fellow at the Industrial Institute for Economic and Social Research, Stockholm (1967–80), at the Arbetslivscentrum (1980–4 and 1986–9), and at the Section of Demography of the University of Stockholm (1984–5). She was a visiting scholar at the University of Colombia in New York, at the Wissenschaftszentrum in Berlin, and at the NORC University of Chicago. She is a member of the Scientific Advisory Board of the European Society for Population Economics (ESPE), Chairperson of the Belle van Zuylen Institute, and member of the Tinbergen Institute. Her main publications are in the area of population economics, human capital and gender, and economics of welfare states and gender.

Barbara Krug has a Ph.D. in Economics at the University of Saarland and has been associate professor (Privatdozentin) at the University of Saarland since 1991. She was a fellow of St Antony's College, Oxford (1987–8) and visiting member at the Institute for Advanced Study, Princeton (1993–4). Her main publications are in the area of public choice, international political economics, new institutional economics, and comparative economic systems. Recent publications include *China's Weg zur Marktwirtschaft*, and *Transformation as Institution Building from Below* (forthcoming).

Danièle Meulders has a Ph.D. in Economics. She is Professor of Economics at the Free University of Brussels and supervisor of the research team on labour economics of the Department of Applied Economics. Her main areas of research include public finance, women's employment, atypical employment and social protection. In collaboration with Robert Plasman and Olivier Plasman, she published *Atypical Employment in the EC*, 1994, Aldershot (Dartmouth).

Janneke Plantenga is lecturer at the Economic Institute of the University of Utrecht. She has a Ph.D in Economics from the University of Groningen. Her main fields of interest are the history of women's work, changing working time patterns and (European) social policy. She is the Dutch member of the European network of experts on the situation of women in the labour market.

Olivier Plasman has a B.A. in Sociology and is a member of the research team on labour economics (ETE) of the Department of Applied Economics of the Free University of Brussels. Together with Danièle Meulders and Robert Plasman, he published *Atypical Employment in the EC*, 1994, Aldershot (Dartmouth).

Robert Plasman has a Ph.D. in Economics. He is Professor of Labour Economics and Human Resources Economics at the Free University of Brussels and supervisor of the research team on labour economics (ETE) of the Department of Applied Economics of the Free University of Brussels. In 1994 he edited *Les Femmes d'Europe sur le Marché du Travail*, Paris (L'Harmattan). In collaboration with Danièle Meulders and Olivier Plasman he published *Atypical Employment in the EC*, 1994, Aldershot (Dartmouth).

Maria Stratigaki studied Economics at the Athens University and Sociology at the University Paris VII and New York University. She obtained a Ph.D. in Labour Sociology at Thessaloniki University. Her areas of research are gender and technology, the impact of computerization on the gender division of labour, and women's work in Southern Europe. Currently she is employed at the Equal Opportunities Unit of the European Commission (DG V).

Dina Vaiou studied Architecture at the National Technical University of Athens, obtained an MA in Planning at UCLA, and did her Ph.D. in Planning at University College, London. She has been assistant professor of urban and regional planning at the National Technical University of Athens since 1982. Previously, she worked freelance in planning and research on urban and regional problems in Greece. She has published on local labour markets and changing forms of production, with an emphasis on gender and women's work, on informal forms of work and subcontracting networks and their impact on spatial development, and on gender divisions in urban space.

Sophia Wunderink-van Veen studied Mathematics at Leiden University and Econometrics at the Erasmus University of Rotterdam. The subject of her Ph.D thesis was the application of budget allocation models for households. From that time on the economic aspects of household behaviour became her main field of interest. In 1990 she published a book on the economics of the household sector (with Aldi Hagenaars, in Dutch). A new book on the same subject will shortly be published in English by Macmillan (now with Peter Kooreman). Although these books and other publications are based on theoretical models, she is well acquainted with the practical side of household behaviour, having a family with five children.

ACKNOWLEDGEMENTS

This book grew out of the wish to introduce the subject of 'gender' into the curriculum of economics. To that aim, a series of lectures started in the early 1990s at the Faculty of Economics and Business Administration of the University of Maastricht. Most of the lectures as well as some additional papers formed the base material for a course in 'Gender and economics', and for this book. For us, both trained as 'conventional' economists, it was an exciting experience to introduce 'gender' in our teaching and to share and exchange views with students.

Many people have contributed to improving the draft chapters. Subsequent cohorts of students of the course 'Gender and economics' at the University of Maastricht used the draft manuscript intensively and made valuable comments. We also benefited from the comments made by Lucia Hanmer, Eddie Pelle, Jacques Siegers, Maarten Vendrik and the anonymous Routledge referees. Marieke Sloep did an excellent job of the drawings, Sen McGlinn was an efficient editor of the English, Karin Scheele performed the tedious task of making a consistent typescript of the different contributions and Jan-Dirk Vlasblom helped fixing many loose ends in the final stage of preparing the manuscript. Finally, we would like to thank the Faculty of Economics and Business Administration of the University of Limburg for their financial contribution to this book.

Geske Dijkstra and Janneke Plantenga
The Hague/Utrecht

1

INTRODUCTION

A. Geske Dijkstra and Janneke Plantenga

The aim of this book is to provide an introduction to gender studies in economics. Currently, this is a rapidly expanding field, and textbooks are urgently necessary. Part I covers important theories, Part II gives an overview of the economic situation of men and women in practice, and Part III examines policies to improve the relative economic situation of women, in particular, affirmative action and comparable worth policies. This book is the first of its kind to take a particularly European perspective.

The reason for editing this volume is our dissatisfaction with the current curriculum. Women have been largely absent as the subject of economic study and still are from mainstream economic textbooks. Theory in economics is often written with a capital T. Theory means model, and model means ideas expressed in mathematical form. This overemphasis on technique and abstract analysis leaves little room for social distinctions like gender (Nelson 1993a, Strassmann 1994). Another shortcoming of the traditional curriculum of economics is that policy questions do not rank high. Many students, trained to uphold the standard of rigour and formal reasoning, have graduated without any knowledge about the actual unemployment level, the pay gap between men and women and the existence of atypical employment. Economists, in the words of McCloskey, enjoy the 'hyperspace of assumptions', but fail to come back to the 'department of economics' (cited in Nelson 1993a: 28). We wanted to get back to the 'department of economics', as it is our contention that the feminist agenda for economics can be most successfully executed if backed by a sound knowledge of empirical data.

For these reasons, this introduction into the field of gender and economics takes place at three different levels. The first level is that of theory. Economic science has been dominated by men, and for that reason economic theory can be expected to suffer from a male bias. A second level is the analysis of the different positions of men and women in the economy, for example the division of labour within the family, the position in the labour market, unequal pay, career possibilities within companies and occupational segregation. This is what we call 'practice' in this book. The

1

third level has to do with European policy. Our attention shifts here towards Brussels and towards the directives, recommendations and action programmes originating there.

According to Ferber and Nelson, 'Gender is the social meaning that is given to biological differences between the sexes; it refers to cultural constructs rather than to biological givens' (Ferber and Nelson 1993: 9–10). By using the word gender, we concentrate on 'the system of social relations that produces distinctions between males and females' (Klamer 1992: 323). This means that biological differences may matter, but we are abstracting from them. The focus on gender in relation to economics implies studying another line of economic research. It differs from mainstream economics in the problems that are selected, the way research takes place and the way findings are interpreted. In the following pages we give an overview of the most important issues in the field of gender and economics, and relate them to the chapters of this book.

FEMINISM AND ECONOMIC THEORIES

Most economists now agree that economic theories have given very little attention to subjects that are important for women, such as the relative position of women in the labour market, and the economic value of household and caring tasks. Economic theory has therefore been biased with respect to the questions that are asked about economic reality. Many feminist economists are also convinced that economics suffers from gender bias with respect to the contents of the theory itself. In order to build theories or models, economists have to simplify reality and create 'stylized facts'. If these stylized facts suffer from gender bias, the theory and models themselves do as well (Woolley 1993). Finally, some feminists argue that a 'feminine' economics will lead to other methods of analysis. The feminist agenda no longer seeks to readjust the content and practice of economics, but tries to transform economics (Ferber and Nelson 1993). With respect to the origin of gender bias in economics, it can be ideology or interest (Seiz 1993). Ideology refers to prevailing ideas about what is feminine and what is masculine; interests are at stake if the organizations or individuals who fund research or who have power over careers influence the type of research that is carried out.

According to the generally accepted definition by Lionel Robbins, economics is the study of how individuals choose among different resources to pursue given ends. This is a very broad definition. Standard economic theories, in particular the dominant neo-classical branch, are narrower in scope and are based on more restrictive assumptions. More recent economic theories, feminist and non-feminist, have attempted to weaken these assumptions and to create theories more in line with observed reality. By highlighting these assumptions and presenting the theoretical responses

2

to them, we may summarize the different theoretical approaches to gender and economic theory as follows (see also Woolley 1993, Seiz 1992, Folbre 1994).

1   The choice between scarce resources is often limited to resources that reach the market-place or that have been defined as 'public' goods or services. The classification of resources into valuable and non-valuable seems somewhat arbitrary.
2   Economics is about the choices of individuals, assuming that each individual has the same objective constraints. Standard neo-classical theory abstracts from the particularities of collective institutions such as families or households, firms, the state, etc. *If* households are taken into account, it is assumed that individuals are completely altruistic within them, while they are pursuing only self-interest in the market-place.
3   Economic theories tend to be static. Many standard theories also often look only at the short-term outcome of an economic model, and disregard long-term effects such as deterioration of the natural environment, or long-term consequences for the distribution of assets in a family or in society at large. In addition, they analyse from a given distribution of economic assets, including both money and power. In this way they conceal conflicts of interest that may exist between members of a family, workers in a firm or contract partners in a market.
4   Economic theories and, in particular, economic methods are based on ideas about what is good science. Good science is usually identified with values that are considered masculine: rationality, abstraction and objectivity. There is less room for values that are traditionally considered feminine, such as irrationality, concreteness and subjectivity (Nelson 1993b).
5   Preferences are usually assumed to be given. Individuals are assumed to be rational, which means that they pursue their own interests. In practice, preferences may be influenced by cultural norms and traditions, collective pressures, interests, ideologies, and also by gender. For example, socialization is different for boys and girls, and cultural norms are different for men and women. As a consequence, preferences may seem to be irrational if only financial costs and benefits are considered.

With respect to the first assumption, more attention is being given to the economic importance of unpaid work in the household and outside the household. Attempts have been made to include household labour and voluntary labour in national economic accounts. Pioneering work in this respect has been done by Waring (1988). Since the non-monetary economy is providing a substantial part of production in less industrialized countries, it is no coincidence that feminist economists get support from development economists (see, for example, Pyatt 1995).

An attempt to include household labour in economic theories began with the work by Nobel Prize winner Gary Becker. He applied standard neo-classical instruments to the distribution of paid and unpaid work within the family (Becker 1965). The 'new home economics', or 'new household economics' is based on his pioneering work. Standard neo-classical theories are applied to explain not only the distribution of paid and unpaid work, but also the amount of human capital (schooling) men and women are investing in themselves, the number of children a couple has, and the amount of human capital they are willing to invest in these children. This new home economics has been heralded as an important new development in economics, proving the richness and flexibility of the neo-classical theory, but has at the same time been condemned as economic imperialism. For feminists, the main criticism seems to be that this research serves to confirm traditional assumptions about the roles of men and women, thereby rationalizing the status quo (Ferber and Nelson 1993: 6; Seiz 1992: 287). Others are less negative and hold the view that the theory is not antifeminist as such; it is only a matter of using it in the right way. The chapter by Wunderink-van Veen is an example of this new approach. Gustafsson in her chapter explicitly refers to this discussion and states: 'using the tools of neo-classical economics with a gender awareness can give us arguments for reforms leading to a society which is at the same time more economically efficient and closer to the vision of a feminist.'

Neo-institutionalist theories deal with the second assumption. They take collectivities and institutions into account. Neo-institutionalist theories deal with three different levels: they analyse the economic consequences of institutions at the macro-economic level; they attempt to explain the organization of exchange and the nature of the contracts (for example in Coase's famous paper on the origin of the firm); and they endogenize social and political rules and the structure of political institutions by analysing costs and benefits for individuals (Eggertsson 1990). Many feminist economists apply a neo-institutionalist framework. They argue that many relations and contracts are not freely negotiable; they are determined by rules and norms. Institutions are given in the short term, and cannot be easily changed. Individuals face constraints, and these constraints are often different for men and women. One can calculate or analyse the costs and benefits of these institutions, and of rules and norms. Krug takes this approach in her chapter.

With respect to the third criticism of standard economic theory, economists now often have a less static view by emphasizing the importance of historical factors and by studying path dependency and hysteresis. The evolutionary school in economics attempts to develop theoretical models in this area. The new growth theory stresses the importance of the initial level of human capital formation and technological development. Some feminists take a more dynamic view while continuing working within the neo-classical tradition. They assume, for instance, that workers become more productive when they are given more demanding jobs; if women are excluded from these more demanding jobs, expectations about productivity of men and women are confirmed. One can also analyse the long-term negative consequences for women of a traditional distribution of paid and unpaid work. In her chapter, Gustafsson gives some examples of this approach.

The fourth criticism has led to different lines of research. One is to question the neutrality and objectivity of economic theories, both by searching for the choices that have been made during the elaboration of certain theories or research, and by close examination of the rhetoric of economics. McCloskey and Klamer question the hegemony of empiricism and positivism in economic science. The use of mathematics, metaphors and of a particular style in economic discourse appears objective but may reflect hidden values, norms and beliefs (Klamer, McCloskey and Solow 1988). Recognizing that the dominant methodology in economics is based on values traditionally considered masculine, such as objectivity and detachment, feminist economists began to search for a more feminine economic methodology. This is the objective of Ferber and Nelson's book, *Beyond Economic Man* (1993). Their plea for 'feminist constructionism' implies the involvement of values traditionally considered feminine, such as dependence and connectedness, instead of or complementary to autonomy and detachment. Nelson (1993a) proposes a new definition of economics as the 'science of provision'. However, it is not yet clear to what kind of economics this new approach leads; as yet, it has not led to a well-developed theoretical alternative (Brown 1994).

Many feminist economists emphasize the need to endogenize preferences, the fifth criticized assumption of standard economic theory (Woolley 1993, Bruyn-Hundt and Kuiper 1994). If women and men are socialized in different ways, so that men attach less value to caring and more to careers, the starting points of partners in a marriage is different; in bargaining models, they have different threatpoints irrespective of purely economic costs and benefits of exit. This means that different utility functions must be taken into account, which is complicated. On a more general level, an interesting attempt to go beyond given preferences has been presented by Folbre (1994). She argues that feminist economic theory must be somewhere in between neo-classical and Marxist theory. The first gives, in her opinion, too much weight to the possibilities for individual choice and for co-ordination, and neglects collective action and conflict. The latter overemphasizes given constraints, conflict and power, and neglects the possibilities for individual agency. Feminist economic theory should look at individuals as 'purposeful agents', who are constrained by 'structures': norms, rules, institutions and the unequal distribution of assets. Preferences, rules, norms and assets all influence behaviour, both individual and collective. Folbre illustrates this broad theoretical framework with an historical analysis of the way caring is organized in different societies. Not surprisingly, her broad hypothesis can explain much more of complex economic developments than a unidimensional framework, be it neo-classical or Marxist. However, much more work remains to be done to establish relations between the different factors, and to assess the relative influence of each factor in specific situations.

THE ECONOMIC POSITION OF WOMEN AND MEN

The second important level of the field of gender and economics is documenting the economic position of men and women. As Woolley (1993) observes, this part of the feminist agenda has advanced much more than the study of feminism and economic theory. Examples include studies of the earnings gap, of discrimination in the labour market, of vertical and horizontal labour market segregation, of the unequal division of unpaid work in the household, and of the extent of female poverty in both industrialized and developing countries. Many good books already exist about the labour market position of women; many of them also attempt to explain the gender differences (Amsden 1980, Bergmann 1986, Blau and Ferber 1986, Kahne and Giele 1992, Folbre et al. 1993). Most of these existing books to date are written from an American standpoint, however, focusing on American facts, institutions, preferences and values. A recent exception is the volume edited by van Doorne-Huiskes, van Hoof and Roelofs (1995), which presents a lot of information on the situation of women in European member states.

A European view within economics is much needed as the European labour market is in many respects an interesting and special case. First, the institutions governing European labour markets are often very different from those in the US. In general, European labour markets are subject to more legal restrictions with respect to labour conditions, rules with respect to hiring and firing, wages and social security. This more active state involvement has a significant impact on employment structures. In the United States, for example, there tends to be a highly polarized labour market in which there are both highly productive and well-paid jobs as well as badly paid and low-productive jobs, the latter especially in the service sector. The absence of a wage policy may even result in wages falling below a socially defined minimum (OECD 1994: 135). In most European countries the wage gap – although growing – is much smaller, and the welfare states provide more employment opportunities for women in particular.

Europe is far from uniform, however. A second reason why Europe is an interesting case to study is that there are large differences between countries in economic structure, economic development, political history and cultural values. This raises questions about how different systems of labour market organization, household organization and state policies shape the distribution of women's activities over paid employment, unemployment, informal employment and domestic and other activities. Third, at the level of the European Union (EU) many attempts have been made to intervene collectively in individual countries' labour markets and welfare states. Success in this 'social area' has so far been limited, but the area of gender policies is an important exception. Finally, Europe includes the so-called countries in transition: the formerly centrally planned economies of Hungary, Poland, the Czech Republic, etc., whose labour markets in transition have special characteristics and problems.

The chapters in Part II provide an overview of women's labour market participation across Europe. The central focus is on the changing patterns of work and working time, giving facts and figures about activity rates, atypical employment and unemployment. The picture which emerges is not wholly positive. There is certainly a rise in women's labour market participation in most countries, but progress seems to have been accompanied by stagnation in the high levels of female unemployment, the wage difference between men and women, and the concentration of women in low-paid, flexible jobs. These labour market inequalities are hard to solve given the current emphasis on flexible labour relations and free, uncontrolled market forces. As a result, the question must be raised whether the increased participation of women through part-time, flexible jobs indicates a real integration, or reflects a new and undesirable segmentation, especially in view of the quality of these jobs.

A common theme in Part II is the importance of unpaid work to explain the unequal position of women in the labour market. Women are more involved than men in caring and household tasks, and for that reason they have less time and energy for paid work outside the household, or for investing in education and training. In turn, the fact that women invest less in education and have lower-paid jobs, forces them to specialize in unpaid work. Obviously, if this kind of circular causation exists, there is not much hope for improvement. A promising line of thought seems to be that both the situation in the labour market and the division of unpaid work are influenced by ideas about what is masculine and what is feminine, in short, gender ideology.

Gender ideology is based on cultural norms and traditions, socialization and expectations. Norms influence the situation of women in the labour market directly, for example by influencing the kind of jobs women can fulfil, but also indirectly by their impact on the organization of paid and unpaid work. Gender ideology creates an implicit 'social contract' with two components, the gender contract and the employment contract (OECD 1994: 19). Within the gender contract women assume most of the unpaid labour, while men are responsible for the financial well-being of the family. This division of labour is reinforced by the employment contract which is based on the sole breadwinner in full-time and lifelong employment.

On a more abstract level, this 'social contract' refers to the institutions of the welfare state. Welfare states, as the work of Esping-Andersen (1990), Lewis (1992) and many others has shown, cannot be seen merely as a passive byproduct of the industrialization process; political priorities and decision-making processes lie at the foundation of these welfare states. Once institutionalized, welfare states make a considerable contribution to maintaining the norms and values associated with the role women (and men) are expected to play, with the division of paid and unpaid work, and with the boundaries between public and private spheres.

Given the strong impact of gender ideology, and the interactions between ideology on the one hand, and institutions and economic structure on the other, it is important to examine these interactions. Normally, this is not done in economics. What is studied is the impact of (changes in) institutions or economic structure on economic behaviour. However, the impact of changes in institutions or in economic structure on gender identities is perhaps even more relevant. This may require more 'subjective' research methods: in-depth case studies instead of large surveys, and interviews instead of questionnaires.

Recently, two such studies have been carried out. Wheelock (1990) studied the impact of a major economic restructuring process in the Wearside region of northeast England on the division of unpaid labour within the household. In this region, since the mid-1970s, employment has shifted from manufacturing to services. This shift was accompanied by a reduction of male, manual jobs in production, and an increase of jobs in services, mainly occupied by women. This brought about high male unemployment rates, while female (part-time) employment increased. Wheelock found that this situation provoked a breaking down of traditional gender roles. Men began to take up much more work in the household. Although some tasks, like ironing, were still performed by women, men came to be responsible for many other domestic chores, such as shopping, cooking and cleaning.

Hochschild (1989) reports on the division of household labour among American couples, in a region that also experienced a reduction of male employment in manufacturing, and an increase of female employment in services. Surprisingly, she found that men who had lower earnings than their female partner contributed less, not more, to household chores. Based on extensive interviews, she concluded that the 'gender identity' of these men had been affected so much by their lower relative earnings, that they compensated by avoiding 'female' (household) work. In families where the men became unemployed, the same occurred. The women in these families experienced a heavy double burden, and were often forced to reduce their working hours outside the home.

From these two studies, two different patterns emerge: the 'Wheelock pattern', according to which the change in economic structure leads to (favourable) changes in gender identities, and the 'Hochschild pattern', according to which gender identities are not changed by material changes. Much more work needs to be done on studying the factors behind these different responses, including the exact male/female distribution of paid and unpaid work before and after the shift in employment structure, government policies regarding welfare, childcare, etc. and the strength of the value framework influencing the ideas on gender identities.

POLICY ISSUES, EQUAL OPPORTUNITIES AND THE EUROPEAN UNION

Part III examines policies to improve the relative labour market position of women. This is another aspect of the feminist agenda, also elaborated in Bergmann (1986). This volume focuses on policies carried out in Europe, in particular the European Union. There are two obvious possibilities for intervention: one is the hiring decision, the other concerns regulations of salaries and other labour conditions (Gustafsson 1991). These two areas are covered in Chapters 9 and 10.

Many more policies can be suggested to improve the economic situation of women in Europe. Given the observed strong interaction between women's labour market position and the economic structure, the institutions of the welfare state, and the division of work within the family, policies in all these areas are important. Examples include increasing childcare provision, possibilities for young parents' leave, and the number of substantial part-time jobs of, for example, thirty-two hours a week, in order to allow for a better 'work–family fit'. A related instrument can be to lower taxes on the provision of personal services. This will both increase the number of jobs that can be performed by (men and) women, and make it easier for working persons to combine household tasks with employed labour. Finally, the distribution of paid and unpaid work within the household can be influenced by attacking stereotyping, particularly in education.

In addition, it is important to have a closer look at the 'general' socio-economic policies advocated by the EU today. How do these policies interfere with the specific position of women and what can be expected from them? Recently, the disappointing evolution of employment led to an intensified interest in the demand side of the labour market; the central question is how the demand for labour can be stimulated. In the proposals put forward thus far, two scenarios can be distinguished: the 'redistribution scenario' and the 'restructuring scenario' (Plantenga 1995). In the latter, growth of the numbers of jobs is central. It plays a prominent role in the White Paper of the former European Commission President Jacques Delors, which advocates an increase of 15 million jobs before the millennium, based on a healthy, open, decentralized, more competitive and fairer economy. Measures to be taken include wage moderation, lifelong training, increasing the flexibility of the labour system and the implementation of trans-European infrastructural projects in the fields of information, transport and energy. The redistribution scenario is intended to complement it. It is not primarily concerned with the creation of more jobs, but with the redistribution of existing work among a larger number of people. The most important instruments are the reduction of working time and the stimulation of part-time employment.

The results of these scenarios in terms of women's future labour market participation may not be altogether favourable. It is likely that women's participation will rise still further, but remain limited to flexible, part-time jobs against a backdrop of high unemployment. One of the main problems seems to be that, although promoting women's labour market participation is a formal aim, equal opportunities' issues are barely included in labour market analyses and labour market policies. As a result, women tend to pay the highest price for the desired flexibility. Given the need to combine paid work with unpaid caring tasks, they opt for a non-standard working time pattern, thus meeting the economy's needs for flexibility. As a result, the insiders–outsiders problem appears to shift. The inequality between people active in the labour market and those who are inactive is replaced by the inequality between those people with good and those with bad jobs.

We can conclude therefore that a restructuring of the European labour market and a redistribution of paid work is necessary, given the high levels of unemployment. The mere creation of jobs, however, will not be sufficient to tackle the inequality between men and women. Men and women face different employment trajectories, with different implications for policy at the European and national levels. To tackle this inequality, more attention should be paid to the compatibility of family responsibilities and labour market participation and the sharing of roles between men and women. This is not an optional development. Indeed, as the Organization for Economic Co-operation and Development (OECD) puts it:

> Ensuring the compatibility of employment and family commitments within individual lives is a major challenge emerging from the process of structural change. Shared family and employment roles will increase the potential labour force, promote a better utilisation of human capital, enhance gender equality and improve quality of life.
>
> (OECD 1994: 19)

SUMMARY OF CHAPTERS

In Part I of this book, we present theories in the area of gender and economics that deal with the first three of the above-mentioned assumptions. Wunderink-van Veen applies neo-classical tools to analyse labour market supply in relation to the presence of children in the household. She explains the basic models of the new home economics, which assume that time spent in household activities is production time, and extends them to allow for investment in human capital and for long-term negative income consequences of a break in participation. She concludes that there are good economic reasons for society to take part of the financial burden of raising children. Her chapter makes clear that the approach of new home economics does not necessarily lead to a confirmation of traditional ideas about the roles of men and women.

Gustafsson presents two examples of generally accepted neo-classical theories, developed by Becker: one on the division of paid and unpaid work within the family, the other on discrimination in the labour market. Both theories confirm traditional ideas about men and women. She then goes on to present two, equally neo-classical, theories on the same subjects developed by female economists, Notburga Ott and Åsa Rosén, respectively. She concludes that although women use the same analytical tools to study these phenomena, the contents of their theories may be different. They are more in keeping with feminist ideas.

Krug provides an example of a neo-institutionalist approach to discrimination. She examines supply and demand in the market for discrimination. On the supply side, five groups of actors have incentives for maintaining discrimination: employers, unions, job incumbents, husbands and political parties. On the demand side, transaction costs, such as mobility costs, scrutiny and uncertainty play a role. In addition, institutions and feedback effects are important. She concludes that there are many economic reasons why discrimination against women can persist, both in the short and in the long term.

In Part II, Meulders, Plasman and Plasman analyse the evolution of two forms of atypical labour market relations in the European Union, part-time employment and temporary employment. An important factor behind this atypical employment in all countries proves to be the general striving for flexibility by employer and employee. The national divergencies are more difficult to explain. Several hypotheses are examined, such as the share of tertiary employment in total employment, the female participation rate, the business cycle and the average wage level.

Plantenga focuses on the labour market position of women on the EU labour market, describing both the European constants and the national particularities. European constants include, for example, lower female activity rates and lower wages for women compared to men. They prove to be related to the unequal distribution of unpaid work between men and women. The national particularities are explained by differences in welfare state regimes. These regimes create different institutional settings, thereby influencing the labour market position of women.

Vaiou and Stratigaki focus on the position of women in Southern EU member states. A large segment of the labour market in these countries can be typified as informal: small family farms, small shops and small enterprises in both production and services. Women are overrepresented in this informal segment of the labour market. This has negative consequences for their earnings and working conditions. To the extent that women are active in the formal labour market, for example in the government, the banking sector or other services, they are often in the lower-paid, part-time and temporary jobs. The authors note that there is less and less attention paid to the regional distribution of welfare within the EU. But even if there is, women are not taken into account: they are not represented in the 'social dialogue' in Brussels.

Dijkstra analyses the position of women in Central and Eastern Europe. During the period of central planning, female labour market participation was almost universal. The state took over many household tasks. Although this reflected a change in official ideology on gender roles, very little changed in the ideas and beliefs concerning male and female roles in and outside the household. As a result, women were absent from higher management and from administrative and technical positions in the labour market. At the same time, women were fully responsible for the household burden. These facts tend to make women particularly vulnerable in the transition to a market economy.

In Part III, van Doorne-Huiskes provides an overview of the policies carried out at the EU level to strengthen the position of women in the labour market. Positive action can be perceived as a powerful instrument of striving for equal opportunities. Although positive action initiatives have been taken in several European countries, the position of women seems hardly improved. The biggest problem seems to be, again, the heavy burden women have in household and caring tasks. The author therefore underlines that actual equality for women and men on the European labour market requires a 'work–family fit'.

De Bruijn focuses on comparable worth and the equal pay policies in the European Union. An important instrument in the struggle for equal pay proves to be a fair system of job evaluation. The unravelling of job evaluation systems, tracing the gender subtext, and tracing the options and decisions of relevant agents in the process, is an important step in revealing the hidden dimension of pay differences between men and women. She also shows that there are many as yet unexplored juridical possibilities to correct unfair job evaluation and pay schemes.

REFERENCES

Amsden, A. (ed.) (1980) *The Economics of Women and Work*, Harmondsworth, Middlesex: Penguin Books.

Becker, G.S. (1965) 'A theory of the allocation of time', *Economic Journal*, 75(299), pp. 493–517.

Bergmann, B.R. (1986) *The Economic Emergence of Women*, New York: Basic Books.

Blau, F. and Ferber, M.A. (1986) *The Economics of Women, Men and Work*, Englewood Cliffs NJ: Prentice Hall.

Brown, V. (1994) 'Feminist constructionism in economics', *The Journal of Economic Methodology*, 1(2), pp. 301–6.

Bruyn-Hundt, M. and Kuiper, E. (1994) 'De vrouw achter de Homo Economicus', *Tijdschrift voor Politieke Ekonomie*, 17(2), pp. 48–62.

Doorne-Huiskes, A. van, Hoof, J. van, and Roelofs, E. (eds) (1995) *Women and the European Labour Markets*, London: Paul Chapman.

Eggertsson, T. (1990) *Economic Behaviour and Institutions*, Cambridge: Cambridge University Press.

Esping-Andersen, G. (1990) *The Three Worlds of Welfare Capitalism*, Cambridge: Polity Press.

Ferber, M.A. and Nelson, J.A. (1993) 'Introduction: the social construction of economics and the social construction of gender', in M.A. Ferber and J.A. Nelson (eds) *Beyond Economic Man: Feminist Theory and Economics*, Chicago and London: University of Chicago Press.

Folbre, N. (1993) 'How does she know? Feminist theories of gender bias in economics', *History of Political Economy*, 25(1), pp. 167–84.

—— (1994) *Who Pays for the Kids? Gender and the Structures of Constraint*, London/New York: Routledge.

——, Bergmann, B., Agarwal, B. and Floro, M. (eds) (1993) *Women's Work in the World Economy*, London: Macmillan.

Gustafsson, S. (1991) 'Half the power, half the incomes and half the glory. The use of microeconomic theory in women's emancipation research', *De Economist*, 139(4), pp. 515–29.

Hochschild, A. (with A. Machung) (1989) *The Second Shift. Working Parents and the Revolution at Home*, New York: Viking.

Kahne, H. and Giele, J.Z. (eds) (1992) *Women's Work and Women's Lives: The Continuing Struggle Worldwide*, Boulder/San Francisco/Oxford: Westview Press.

Klamer, A. (1992) 'Commentary', in N. de Marchi (ed.) *Post-Popperian Methodology of Economics*, Boston: Kluwer Academic Publishers.

——, McCloskey, D.N. and Solow, R.M. (eds) (1988) *The Consequences of Economic Rhetoric*, New York: Cambridge University Press.

Lewis, J. (1992) 'Gender and the development of welfare regimes', *Journal of European Social Policy*, 2(3), pp. 159–73.

Nelson, J.A. (1993a) 'The study of choice or the study of provisioning? Gender and the definition of economics', in M.A. Ferber and J.A. Nelson (eds) *Beyond Economic Man: Feminist Theory and Economics*. Chicago/London: University of Chicago Press.

—— (1993b) 'Gender and economic ideologies', *Review of Social Economy*, 51(3), pp. 287–301.

OECD (1994) 'Shaping structural change. The role of women', in OECD, *Women and Structural Change. New Perspectives*, Paris: OECD.

Plantenga, J. (1995) 'Labour-market participation of women in the European Union', in A. van Doorne-Huiskes, J. van Hoof, and E. Roelofs (eds) *Women and the European Labour Markets*, London: Paul Chapman.

Pyatt, G. (1995) *Balanced Development*, Inaugural address, The Hague: Institute of Social Studies.

Seiz, J. (1992) 'Gender and economic research', in N. de Marchi (ed.) *Post-Popperian Methodology of Economics*, Boston: Kluwer Academic Publishers.

—— (1993) 'Feminism and the history of economic thought', *History of Political Economy*, 25(1), pp. 185–201.

Strassmann, D.L. (1994) 'Feminist thought and economics; or what do the Visigoths know', *American Economic Review*, 84(2), pp. 153–8.

Waring, M.J. (1988) *If Women Counted: A Feminist Economics*, New York/San Francisco: Harper.

Wheelock, J. (1990) *Husbands at Home: The Domestic Economy in a Post-Industrial Society*, London/New York: Routledge.

Woolley, F.R. (1993) 'The feminist challenge to neoclassical economics', *Cambridge Journal of Economics*, 17(1), pp. 485–500.

Part I
THEORIES

2

NEW HOME ECONOMICS: CHILDREN AND THE LABOUR MARKET PARTICIPATION OF WOMEN

Sophia Wunderink-van Veen

INTRODUCTION

In this chapter, micro-economic models are used to analyse the relation between the labour market participation of women and the presence of children in a household. Economic theory can help to explain the labour supply of men and women, their participation rates, their wish for part-time jobs and the need for (subsidized) professional childcare centres. It may also help to increase the understanding of policy makers, employers and (potential) employees themselves, so that they can develop strategies for reaching their targets. The labour supply models are based on the neo-classical model of consumer behaviour. We will use this model only as a starting point. It is quite restrictive and not sophisticated enough to explain the relation between the presence of children and female labour supply.

In this chapter we start with a short exposition of the neo-classical model of labour supply, followed by Becker's household production model. Both models describe the choices of one-person households. The next step is to analyse a multi-person household, through a model for a two-person household. This model allows for three different kinds of time use: paid labour, household labour and leisure. The optimal division of labour between household members depends on their relative wage rates. However, wage rates are not constant over time, but are affected by changes in human capital. So, we have to consider the relation between wage rates and human capital. Many people like to have children. The presence of children in a household will change preferences. Therefore we introduce an economic model in which the number and 'quality' of children appear as arguments in the utility function of the parents. It is a static, one-period model. But as households can also make choices with respect to the timing of the births of their children, the next step is to consider the behaviour of households with respect to labour market participation and the timing of births. The chapter concludes with a short summary of the main results.

LABOUR SUPPLY IN THE NEO-CLASSICAL MODEL

In the neo-classical model it is assumed that the rational consumer has full information on prices and quality of goods and services, on income and on wage rates. The consumer's preferences can be represented by a utility function. Utility is not only provided by goods and services but also by leisure time. The consumer makes choices to maximize utility. The model looks like this:

Maximize $U(x_1, \ldots, x_n, T_l)$
subject to: $T = t_l + t_w$
  $Y \geqslant p_1 x_1 + \ldots + p_n x_n$
  $Y = Y_0 + wt_w$

---

where:

x_n	= quantity good n	t_l	= leisure time
p_n	= price of good n	t_w	= labour time
Y	= total income	w	= the consumer's wage rate
Y_0	= non-wage (unearned) income	n	= 1, . . ., N

In a more compact form the model looks like this:

Maximize $U(C, t_l)$
subject to: $[w(T-t_l) + Y_0]/p = C$

---

where:

C = consumption
p = price index of consumption

The left-hand side of the restriction represents real household income. The restriction is often presented as a full income restriction:

$$wT + Y_0 = pC + wt_l$$

The optimal choice of the consumer between consumption and leisure determines his or her optimal labour supply. The model is illustrated by Figure 2.1.

The slope α of the budget line AB in Figure 2.1 is determined by the real wage rate w/p. The optimal choice S depends on the shape of the utility function, on the real wage rate and on non-wage (unearned) income. If the wage rate increases, it may cause a change in labour supply. Since full income $(wT+Y_0)$ rises, the demand for consumption and leisure will increase (income effect), but the opportunity costs of leisure will increase as well, while the price of consumption is supposed to remain constant. Therefore the substitution effect of a wage increase is a decrease in demand

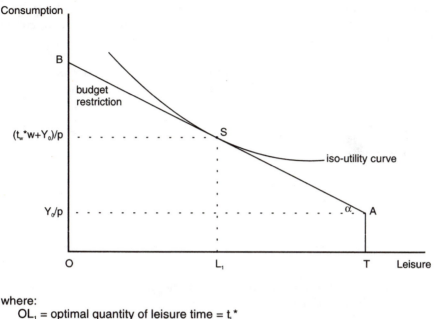

Figure 2.1 The choice between consumption and leisure

for leisure. The total effect on demand for leisure and thus on labour supply is unknown: it depends on the strength of the income and substitution effects. If the substitution effect is stronger than the income effect, the result of a wage rate increase will be an increase in labour supply. However, as soon as the income effect becomes stronger than the substitution effect the result will be reversed.

In the neo-classical model, the wage rate is an exogenous variable; i.e., the consumer has no influence on his or her own wage rate. This may be true in the short term, but certainly not in the long term. It is one of the non-realistic features of this model. We will return to this point later on.

LABOUR SUPPLY IN 'THE NEW HOME ECONOMICS' MODEL

In 1965, Gary Becker published his famous article in which time spent on household production was introduced as an alternative for leisure. His big innovation is that activities in the household are not considered as leisure, but as productive activities. In Becker's model, utility depends on the commodities people consume. These commodities are produced in the household with household labour time and market goods. The household adds value to the market products. The production processes are described by production functions.

In the neo-classical model there are two kinds of time use: paid labour and leisure. In Becker's model there is a distinction between paid labour and various kinds of household labour. This provides new insights into the household's allocation of time and money. The model looks like this:

Maximize $U(z_1, \ldots, z_n)$
subject to:
$$Y = Y_0 + wt_w$$
$$z_n = f_n(x_n, t_n) \qquad n=1, \ldots, N$$
$$Y \geqslant p_1x_1 + \ldots + p_Nx_N$$
$$T = \sum_{n=1}^{N} t_n + t_w$$

where:

z_n = quantity of home-produced commodity n
f_n = production function for commodity n
t_n = household labour time for the production of n

Figure 2.2 shows what a household production function could look like, for a fixed amount of market goods. The marginal product of household labour, the slope of AB, is positive but decreasing.

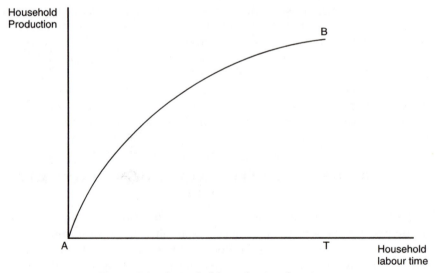

Figure 2.2 A household production function

Since this is a static model designed to describe the economic behaviour of one person with only two kinds of time use, it is still quite restrictive. In Becker's model all household activities are described by production functions. Some activities that are treated as productive home production activities, are in fact pure leisure, like watching a film on television. Other activities should be considered as investment activities, for example going to school.

An extension of Becker's model is introduced by Gronau (1980). Gronau distinguishes three types of time use: paid labour, household labour and leisure. There are also some simplifications introduced:

1 There are only three commodities, z_1, z_2 and z_3.
   $z_1 = f_1 (t_L) = t_L$, pure leisure
   $z_2 = f_2 (x) = x$, market consumption goods
   $z_3 = f_3 (t_h)$, household production
   Commodity z_1 is leisure, no market goods are involved; commodity z_2 consists only of market goods, no household labour time is needed; and commodity z_3 represents household production. It is assumed here that no market goods are needed in the household production process.
2 The commodities z_2 and z_3 are supposed to be perfect substitutes. The total quantity $(z_2 + z_3)$ appears in the utility function, since the consumer is supposed not to prefer one over the other.

So, the model becomes:

$$
\begin{aligned}
&\text{Maximize } U(z_1, z_2 + z_3) \\
&\text{subject to:} \quad Y_0 + wT = t_L w + t_h w + px \\
&\qquad\qquad\quad z_3 = f_3(t_h) \\
&\qquad\qquad\quad z_2 = x \\
&\qquad\qquad\quad z_1 = t_L \\
&\qquad\qquad\quad T = t_w + t_L + t_h
\end{aligned}
$$

By making these assumptions it becomes possible to represent this model in a two-dimensional diagram, as shown in Figures 2.3a and 2.3b. The consumer's optimal choice of time allocation depends on his or her preferences (the shape of the iso-utility curve), the individual's wage rate, prices and the shape of the household production function.

In Figures 2.3a and 2.3b the curve TABC represents the border of the area from which the consumer can choose. Part AB shows the household production function. It would continue beyond B, but at point B the marginal product of household labour equals the marginal product of market activities, and to the left of B the marginal product of market activities will be greater than the marginal product of household activities. Since household production and market goods are supposed to be perfect

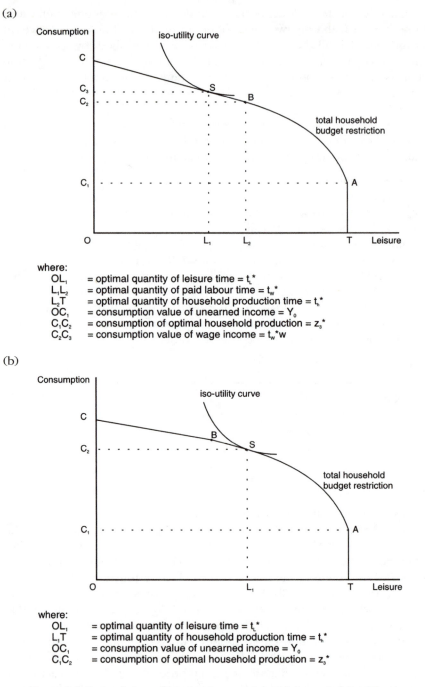

where:
OL_1 = optimal quantity of leisure time = t_L^*
L_1L_2 = optimal quantity of paid labour time = t_w^*
L_2T = optimal quantity of household production time = t_h^*
OC_1 = consumption value of unearned income = Y_0
C_1C_2 = consumption of optimal household production = z_3^*
C_2C_3 = consumption value of wage income = $t_w^* w$

where:
OL_1 = optimal quantity of leisure time = t_L^*
L_1T = optimal quantity of household production time = t_h^*
OC_1 = consumption value of unearned income = Y_0
C_1C_2 = consumption of optimal household production = z_3^*

Figure 2.3 Optimal time allocation in a model with household production

substitutes, the best opportunities for the consumer continue along the line BC, the slope of which equals the real market wage rate (w/p). The optimal choice of the consumer, point S, can either be such that time is allocated over three activities: leisure, paid labour and household production (Figure 2.3a); or over two activities: leisure and household production (Figure 2.3b).

If the wage rate increases, the probability of labour market participation increases, since point B will shift to the right (in the direction of A) and less time will be spent on household production. Moreover, both the opportunity costs of leisure and of household production increase for a working consumer. The income effect of a wage increase has a positive effect on all 'normal' commodities and the substitution effect causes a shift to less time-intensive activities. If the household production process becomes more efficient, the production curve AB will become steeper and point B will shift to the left. Less time is needed to produce the same amount of commodities at home. But, due to the substitution effect, demand for home-produced commodities may increase and it is impossible to predict the effect on total time use.

HOUSEHOLDS CONSISTING OF MORE THAN ONE PERSON

Two persons forming a household share total income and total household production in a way that suits them best. Although differences in the preferences and power of the household members are very interesting, for simplicity's sake we suppose here that the household members have one common utility function (see Ott's model in Chapter 3 of this volume for the importance of differences in preferences and 'power'). The two household members may have different market wage rates and different household productivity. In these circumstances it is obvious that both partners can benefit from a certain division of labour between them. Only comparative advantages are important. Suppose the wife's comparative advantage for labour market work over household production is w^1/g^1 and the husband's comparative advantage is w^2/g^2.

$$g^i = \frac{\partial f}{\partial t_h{}^i} = \text{marginal household productivity of } i$$

w^i = market wage rate of i, $i = 1, 2$

Then if $w^1/g^1 > w^2/g^2$ for $t_h{}^1 = t_h{}^2$, the optimal household choice will result in a division of labour such that the wife $(i=1)$ spends more hours in the labour market than her partner, and the husband will spend more hours on household production and less in the labour market. The model becomes:

Maximize $U(z, t_L^1, t_L^2)$
subject to:
$$z = f(x, t_h^1, t_h^2)$$
$$T = t_w^1 + t_h^1 + t_L^1$$
$$T = t_w^2 + t_h^2 + t_L^2$$
$$Y_0 + t_w^1 w^1 + t_w^2 w^2 = px$$

In the optimum, the ratio of the marginal household productivities of the two partners equals the ratio of their market wage rates. If partner 1 has a higher wage rate than partner 2, $w^1 > w^2$, then $\dfrac{\partial f}{\partial t_h^1}$ must be greater than $\dfrac{\partial f}{\partial t_h^2}$ and if the household production functions of the partners are the same, it follows from Figure 2.2 that this is only possible if partner 1 spends less time on household production than partner 2.

An important aspect omitted from the analysis is the utility or disutility of the activities themselves. In Winston (1982) a model is introduced in which these two kinds of utilities are taken into account. For instance, the commodity produced when cleaning the house is 'a clean house' and we assume that the person involved appreciates a clean house. A second point is whether the activity, cleaning, is appreciated or not. This will influence the utility stream per time unit. So besides differences in productivity between the partners, there may be differences in the appreciation (utility) of the activities themselves. This will affect the joint utility function of the household, which may consist of a weighted average of the two separate utility functions. A second limitation of the model is that w^1 and w^2 are supposed to be fixed, while in practice they are not. In the next section we will consider this point.

WAGE RATE AND INVESTMENT IN HUMAN CAPITAL

Thus far we have used only static one-period models. This means that the optimal division of labour between partners, as found above, is only a short-term optimum. Long-term consequences of these choices are not taken into account: specialization, though optimal in the short term, may lead to unwanted dependency in the long term (Hagenaars and Wunderink-van Veen 1990). Therefore it is important to study the determinants of the wage rate and a person's earning capacity over his or her life span.

The market wage rate of a person depends on many variables and it is certainly not constant over time. One of the variables on which it depends is the amount of human capital that is accumulated in a person. A child starts building up human capital from the day it is born, by learning at home, at school, and finally in a paid job. The latter learning can take the forms of on-the-job training and the accumulation of experience. When people enter the labour market, their wage rates are unequal, due to different amounts of human capital. One can try to increase one's wage rate by adding human capital through going to university or taking courses).

Some typical age-earning profiles are shown in Figure 2.4, in which the lower curve represents a person with lower education. This person starts working at age A_1, say $A_1=16$. An individual who successfully continues education for some years will enter the labour market at a higher age, say $A_2=23$, but total lifetime income, represented by the total area under the curve, up to $A_3 = 65$, is greater.

The assumption is that

$$w_t = f(H_t)$$

where:

H_t = the individual's amount of human capital, period t.

H_t itself depends on the amount of human capital with which the person entered the labour market H_1, and on the net investments in human capital from period 1 to period t.

$$H_2 = (1-\delta)H_1 + I_1$$
$$H_3 = (1-\delta)H_2 + I_2$$
$$\vdots \qquad \qquad \vdots$$
$$\vdots \qquad \qquad \vdots$$
$$H_t = (1-\delta)H_{t-1} + I_{t-1}$$

where:

δ = depreciation rate of human capital

I_τ = investment in human capital in period τ, $\tau=1, \ldots, t$

Therefore $H_t = f(H_1, I_1, \ldots, I_{t-1}, \delta)$, and as long as $\delta H_\tau < I_\tau$, human capital will increase and w_t will increase. So age-income profile curves are usually rising, because work experience prevents obsolescence and deterioration of human capital. On-the-job training and work experience can be seen as net investments. If investments are lacking, the curves no longer rise. Human capital, like physical capital, suffers from obsolescence. People forget the knowledge or skills they do not use for some time, and their knowledge becomes outdated.

For some people the typical age-earning profile of Figure 2.4 is interrupted because they withdraw temporarily from the labour market at age A_i, as in Figure 2.5. The withdrawal is sometimes caused by labour market circumstances leading to unemployment. In other cases it concerns women who withdraw from the labour market because of the birth of a child. Their working career is interrupted either because they prefer to stay at home with their young children, or because professional childcare is not available or is too expensive. Income reduces to the level Y_0 of non-wage income (social security benefits, the income of a partner or child benefits). When they re-enter the labour market at age A_r, their wage rate is usually less than when they left the labour market.

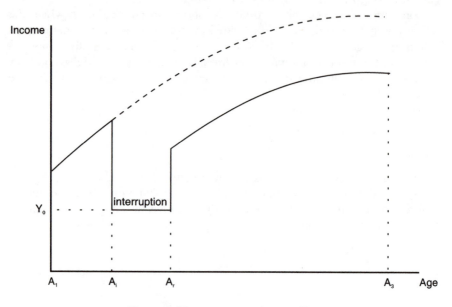

Y_0

interruption

A_1 A_i A_r A_3 Age

Figure 2.4 Some age-earning profiles

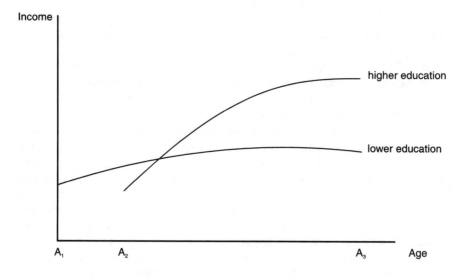

Figure 2.5 Age-earning profile, interrupted career

HOUSEHOLD TIME ALLOCATION AND CHILDREN

The presence of children in a household is expected to cause a change in the optimal choices, with respect to both expenditures and labour supply. The neo-classical models usually consider only alterations in the allocation of the household budget, but since the budget is not an exogenous variable, time allocation should be studied together with expenditure allocation. This section outlines a static model which can be used to analyse the optimal choices of households with children. We will start again with one of Becker's models. 'Childcare' can be considered as one of the commodities produced with household labour and market goods. Children cost time and money. On the other hand we assume that it is the parents' choice to have children (the statistical validity of this assumption will of course vary in different cultures, and within each culture between the genders). Children give love, pleasure, satisfaction, things that an economist would call utility. So children should be mentioned in their parents' utility function. Usually a distinction is made between the number of children in a household and the 'quality' (Becker 1981, Nerlove, Razin and Sadka 1987):

$$u = U(z, n, q)$$

where:

z = household commodities
n = number of children
q = 'quality' offered to each child

It is assumed that $\Delta U/\Delta n$ is positive, keeping q and z constant. This does not contradict the fact that, in this century, increasing incomes are observed together with a continuous decrease in family size. At first glance this is similar to the consumption pattern of 'inferior goods'. But in the case of children, it is not only the number of children which is important: the care, the attention, the education and material goods provided to them also determine their utility for the parents. So $\delta U/\delta q > 0$. In economic terms, 'childcare' is offered with a combination of time and money. Parents must choose whether they will offer their 'childcare' to a large number of children, or to a small number. If they choose to have a large number of children, the amount of childcare available to each child will be small, since both income and time are limited. The amount of childcare available for each child is what is called the 'quality' of a child. During this century the possibility of choice was created by the introduction of contraceptives. What we observe is that parents prefer 'quality' over 'number'.

An important factor in the analysis is that time and money can, to a certain extent, be substituted in the production of 'childcare'. Crèches, day-care centres and private nannies can replace the parents, but they have to be paid. These are the market goods that can be considered as substitutes for parents' care. Iso-quality curves are drawn in Figure 2.6. Higher quality is represented by a greater quantity of market goods and/or more parental time per child.

An extension of Becker's model consists of the following equations:

$$\text{Maximize } U(z, n, q, t_L^1, t_L^2)$$
$$\text{subject to:} \qquad z = f_h(x, t_h^1, t_h^2)$$
$$qn = f_{ch}(x_{ch}, t_{ch}^1, t_{ch}^2)$$
$$T = t_w^1 + t_h^1 + t_{ch}^1 + t_L^1$$
$$T = t_w^2 + t_h^2 + t_{ch}^2 + t_L^2$$
$$Y_0 + t_w^1 w^1 + t_w^2 w^2 = px + p_{ch}x_{ch}$$

where:

q = quality per child
n = number of children
f_{ch} = household production function of childcare
t_{ch}^i = time input for the production of childcare, partner i, i = 1, 2
f_h = household production function of other commodities
t_L^i = leisure time of partner i, i = 1, 2

This model provides an optimal choice for n and q, but also for the labour supply of both partners: t_w^1 and t_w^2. Since production functions f_n and f_{ch} allow for substitution between time and market goods, both parents may choose labour market participation, one of them may withdraw from the

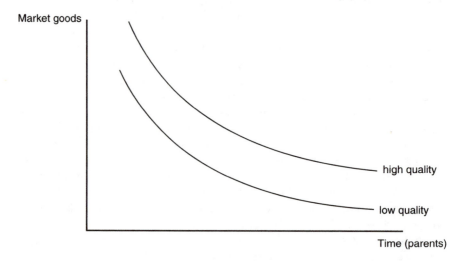

Figure 2.6 Childcare iso-quality lines allowing for substitution between parental care and market childcare

labour market, or both of them may choose part-time jobs. In a way this is still a rather restricted model, because it is static and no attention is paid to the development of human capital of the parents. On the other hand, this is a model in which the amount of human capital of the children is explicitly considered. The quality variable q is comparable with the H_1 variable of the former section.

The effect of the presence of children on the age-earning profile and the expenditures of the household is shown in Figures 2.7 and 2.8. In Figure 2.7 it is assumed that both partners keep their jobs after the birth of their children. During the period that the children live with their parents, expenditures rise. Not only do the parents have to buy extra goods for their children (a cost which rises over time), they also have to buy 'childcare', especially in the pre-school period. The cost of professional childcare is far from negligible.

If one of the parents withdraws from the labour market, both income and expenditures decrease, as compared to the situation in Figure 2.7. But as was suggested in Figure 2.5, re-entering the labour market is often quite problematic and earnings are less than before (Mincer and Ofek 1982, Moffitt 1984). The long-term consequences of a complete withdrawal from the labour market are less favourable than the short-term solution the Becker model would suggest. The difference between total income and expenditures after re-entering the labour market is usually less favourable than in the situation outlined in Figure 2.8.

A special case is that of one-parent families. There is no second income

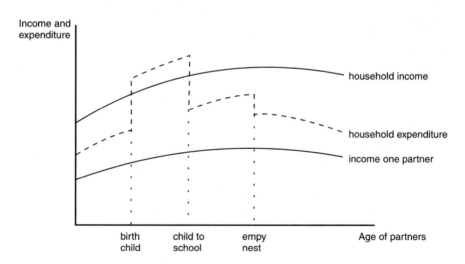

Figure 2.7 Household life-cycle earning and expenditure profiles, both partners having equally paid, full-time jobs

29

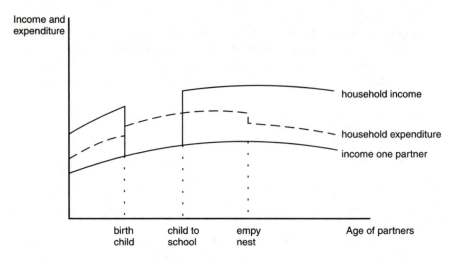

Figure 2.8 Household life-cycle earning and expenditure profiles, with interrupted working career of one of the partners

and the parent has only twenty-four hours a day available for paid labour, home production, childcare and leisure. If the parent's level of education is low, the labour market will offer only a low salary and unattractive work. In that case, taking care of the children with only a social security income and child benefits is often chosen as the optimal solution. This situation is represented in Figure 2.9. If the parent does not have a job and receives child benefits plus social security, income is C_0^{nw}. The household production function DPE determines the total household budget line TDPE. The utility maximizing choice is point P.

If the parent finds a job and loses the social security benefits, income will be $C_0 + (C_1^w - C_2^w)$, which is usually more than C_0^{nw}. The household production function ABF is identical to DPE, but on BF the marginal product of household production is less than the market wage rate. So, paid labour opens more consumption opportunities than household production and the total household budget line in this case is TABSC and the utility maximizing point is S. However, Figure 2.9 shows that the utility level at P is higher than at S, so here P is the optimal choice. The situation will change when either the parent's wage rate becomes higher (and the curve BC becomes steeper), or when the social security benefit decreases, that is when point D is lower. Then labour market participation may become the optimal choice.

THE TIMING OF BIRTHS

Since knowledge about contraception has become general, and contra-

30

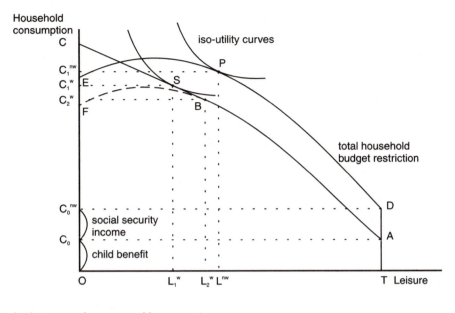

In the case of a non-working parent:

OL^{nw}	= optimal quantity of leisure
$L^{nw}T$	= optimal quantity of household production time (including childcare)
OC_0	= consumption value of child benefit
$C_0C_0^{nw}$	= consumption value of social security income
$C_0^{nw}C_1^{nw}$	= consumption value of household production

In the case of a working parent:

OL_1^w	= optimal quantity of leisure
$L_1^wL_2^w$	= optimal quantity of parent labour time
L_2^wT	= optimal quantity of household production time
OC_0	= consumption value of child benefit
$C_0C_2^w$	= consumption value of household production
$C_2^wC_1^w$	= consumption value of wage income

Figure 2.9 One-parent household choice between labour market participation and social security

ceptives are easy to obtain, low-priced and socially accepted, we assume that people can make the decision not to have a child. The positive choice cannot always be realized. The partners choose the best period for a birth, taking into account their whole life cycle, the effect of the presence of children on their earning capacities, and the time and financial costs of children. In the theoretical model incorporating these factors, parents are assumed to maximize utility over their whole life spans. The life cycle consists of a limited number of periods, as in Figures 2.7 and 2.8. Present and future consumption, together with the number and 'quality' of children, determine the utility level:

Maximize U(C, B)

where:

C = a consumption index
B = a fertility index

C depends on the appreciation of consumption during each period, so

$$C = \sum_{t=1}^{T} u_t(C_t)$$

B depends on the number of children and the time and money that are invested in the children:

$$B = \sum_{t=1}^{T} v_t(I_t)B_t$$

where:

B_t = birth rate at time t
B_t = 0 in the periods before the birth of the first child and after the children have left home
B_t = number of children born in period t
I_t = amount of money invested in a child, born in period t

The amount of time that is needed to raise a child is used as the unit of time. So for B_t children the parents need B_t time units. The fertility index B is an indicator of the amount of time and money invested in children. It is assumed that the parent's limited energy E can be used to earn money in the labour market and to raise children. Only the difference between E and B remains as labour supply:

$S_t = E - B_t$
E = work capacity of parent

Both S_t, E and B_t are expressed in time units mentioned above.

The wage rate of the parent in period t depends on the parent's stock of human capital at the beginning of that period: H_t. Human capital grows with the working experience of the parent, which can be considered as investments in human capital, so

$$H_t = H_1 + \beta \sum_{\tau=1}^{t-1} S_\tau$$

The wage rate depends on H_t, so $w_t = f(H_t)$. Here we assume proportionality:

$$w_t = \omega H_t$$

The life cycle model, with the timing of births, now becomes

Maximize U (C,B)

subject to: $\displaystyle\sum_{t=1}^{T}(C_t + (I_t - Y^0)B_t)r^{-t} \leqslant A + \sum_{t=1}^{T}S_t w_t r^{-t}$

---

where:

A = A_1 + present value of the partner's earning during $t = 1, \ldots, T$
A_1 = assets at the beginning of period 1
Y^0 = child benefit rate.
r = a discount rate

The left-hand side of the restriction equals the present value of expenditures over the life cycle of an individual, the right-hand side represents the present value of the income flow. So the restriction is an inter-temporal budget constraint.

Until the first child is born, $S_t = E$ and human capital grows:

$$H_t = H_1 + \beta\sum_{\tau=1}^{t-1}E$$

If B_t children are born in period t, $H_{t+1} = H_t + \beta(E - B_t)$.

The difference in human capital between having no children and having B_t children is βB_t and the corresponding difference in wage rate is $\omega\beta B_t$. From this it follows that the cost of having B_t children in period t becomes:

$$B_t(I_t - Y^0) + B_t w_t + \beta\omega\sum_{\tau=t+1}^{T}B_t r^{t-\tau}$$

and the cost per child is:

$$p_t = (I_t - Y^0) + w_t + \beta\omega\sum_{\tau=t+1}^{T}r^{t-\tau}$$

The cost is the sum of three terms: $(I_t - Y^0)$ indicates the financial burden of a child born in period t; w_t is the opportunity cost of the time that is needed to raise a child during period t (remember that the time unit is the amount of time needed to raise a child and the dimension of w_t is wage amount/time unit); and $\beta\omega\sum\limits_{\tau=t+1}^{T}r^{t-\tau}$ is the present value of the costs due to the loss (or lack of growth) of human capital. From this it follows that postponing births raises income losses $B_t w_t$ during the 'child period', but diminishes income losses associated with capital loss after the 'child period' $\beta\omega\sum\limits_{\tau=t+1}^{T}r^{t-\tau}$.

CONCLUSION

The 'new home economics' theory provides a very important framework for the analysis of household behaviour. The different ways in which time can be used, for productive (paid or unpaid) work, recreation, or investment make household choices complicated. There is always a short-term and a long-term effect of a time-use decision, and what is optimal in the short term is not necessarily optimal for the long term. A good example of this is the division of labour between partners in the presence of children. In the short term, changes in human capital and long-term earning capacity are neglected, but in the long-term analysis it is very common to neglect the short-term joy of raising one's own children. To summarize, the economic models predict that:

1 The probability of labour market participation increases as the wage rate increases.
2 The higher the wage rate, the more hours are spent in the labour market. However, at a certain level, an increase in wage rate may result in a decrease in the labour supply due to the income effect.
3 The quality of work in better-paid jobs is usually higher, because more human capital is required and jobs become more interesting. This adds extra utility to labour market participation.
4 If the optimal division of labour between partners leads to extreme specialization, which means that one of the partners spends as much time in the labour market as possible and the other in the household, the long-term effect is that the wage rate of the 'working' partner increases and the wage rate of the other decreases. The result in the long term may be an unwanted dependency.
5 The more children there are in a family, the more 'efficient' it becomes to raise the children at home, due to economies of scale.
6 The long-term effect of a withdrawal from the labour market is a loss of human capital for the parent. In the meantime this parent is investing in the human capital of the child, by offering 'quality' to the child. However, quality can also be offered with professional childcare.
7 The lower the price of professional childcare and the better the quality, the higher the probability of labour market participation of the parents and the greater the number of hours worked.

8 The human capital variable can explain long-term effects of labour market decisions and timing of births.

These are hypotheses that should be tested with real data.

None of these models considers the fact that children are a joint responsibility of the private household and society. In economic models, children are often compared with (private) durable goods, but it is less common to compare them with public goods. In the Netherlands, the government provides free school education to the age of 16, and subsidizes higher education to a great extent. Students receive scholarships and all families with children younger than 18 receive child benefits, independent of their incomes. All these measures have the effect of government taking away from parents part of the financial burden of raising children.

The reason for this is that society as a whole benefits from the human capital stock of all its members. If the education of children was a purely private matter, some households might not be able to provide enough care and material goods to build up the children's human capital. In the long run this would mean that the labour market would not be supplied with enough skilled labour and total national production would suffer. In the United States, the government is less involved with private households and their welfare. The results of that policy are described in Hewlett's book *When the Bough Breaks* with the revealing subtitle *The Cost of Neglecting our Children*.

REFERENCES

Becker, G.S. (1965) 'A theory of the allocation of time', *Economic Journal*, 75(299), pp. 493–517.

—— (1964) *Human Capital*, New York: National Bureau of Economic Research.

—— (1981) *A Treatise on the Family*, Cambridge, Mass.: Harvard University Press.

Gronau, R. (1980) 'Home production, a forgotten industry', *The Review of Economics and Statistics*, 62(3), pp. 408–16.

Hagenaars, A.J.M. and Wunderink-van Veen, S.R. (1990) *Soo Gewonne, Soo Verteert, Economie van de Huishoudelijke Sector*, Leiden: Stenfert Kroese.

Hewlett, S.A. (1991) *When the Bough Breaks: the Cost of Neglecting our Children*, New York: Basic Books.

Mincer, J. and Ofek, H. (1982) 'Interrupted work careers: depreciation and restoration of human capital', *The Journal of Human Resources*, 18(1), pp. 3–24.

Moffitt, R. (1984) 'Profiles of fertility, labour supply and wages of married women: a complete life cycle model', *Review of Economic Studies*, 51(2), pp. 263–78.

Nerlove, M., Razin, A. and Sadka, E. (1987) *Household and Economy: Welfare Economics of Endogenous Fertility*, London: Academic Press.

Winston, G.C. (1982) *The Timing of Economic Activities*, Cambridge: Cambridge University Press.

3

FEMINIST NEO-CLASSICAL ECONOMICS: SOME EXAMPLES[1]

Siv Gustafsson

INTRODUCTION

Feminism is likely to change economic theory. However, one can have different views on how this change is going to come about. One view is to refute neo-classical theory and argue that there is a need for alternative feminist economics.

A second view is to argue that by applying the feminist perspective to an existing economic theory, different policy implications will be drawn. A third view is to argue that feminist economists will improve neo-classical theory by removing its male bias and thereby may reveal mechanisms through which the overall efficiency of the economy could be increased.

I do not share the first view, but I agree with the second view for the following reasons. Recent developments in economic theory have contributed to the understanding of women's position in the economy. The pioneers in extending neo-classical theory into fields of interest for the study of women's position in the economy are primarily Gary Becker (1957, 1964) and Jacob Mincer (1962, 1974). The field is often referred to as the economics of the family (Schultz 1974, Cigno 1991) or economics of the household (Hagenaars and Wunderink-van Veen 1990). Through the development of this theory we can analyse issues such as wage differentials between women and men, discrimination in labour markets, division of work within the family, fertility decisions, the effects of work interruptions on career development and the effect of day-care subsidies on women's labour supply.

Different policy implications can be derived from the same economic model, and this is what the second view implies. In relation to women's often interrupted careers, the human capital model can be interpreted to indicate that only childless women can count on a career development equal to men even in the absence of discrimination (Mincer and Polachek 1974). But the same result can also be interpreted in a feminist way to argue for subsidized childcare to enable mothers to combine work and family rather than interrupt their careers (Gustafsson 1984, 1991).

In this chapter I want to go one step further and argue that the male bias in economics may conceal important economic mechanisms, and this in turn may lead to policy recommendations which are less economically efficient (the third view). Efficiency is at the heart of economic analysis. Sometimes a more equal distribution of income between different members of society can be shown to be equally efficient, but often there is a trade-off between efficiency and equality (cf. Layard and Walters 1978: Chapter 1). Analysis of feminist goals can then be framed in terms of this trade-off between efficiency and equality (cf. Cain 1985).

A more fundamental contribution of feminists to neo-classical theory would be to show that the theory which has been built up has arrived at conclusions implying suboptimal behaviour because of a lack of gender awareness. The theoretical work of two female economists has convinced me that this can sometimes be the case. Notburga Ott (1992) shows that even if the division of work and trade is optimal in the short run as Becker (1981: Chapter 2) predicts, it is not optimal in a long-term perspective because it implies decreasing power and outside options for the partner specializing in household production, and that a suboptimal number of children will therefore be born. The decision to have a child is analysed as a prisoner's dilemma in Ott's (1992) model.

Åsa Rosén (1993) employs a matching model based on the search theory literature (cf. Pissarides 1990). She shows that, based on the economic mechanism of matching between jobs and workers, the presence of discrimination will lead to suboptimal matches with losses of economic efficiency as a result. She also shows that discrimination will not disappear because the discriminatory equilibrium is stable, and affirmative action may be needed to bring about a more efficient non-discriminatory equilibrium.

In this chapter, I will first discuss the definitions of neo-classical economic theory and feminism. In the next sections I will contrast Gary Becker's (1981) model of the division of work within the family with that of Notburga Ott (1992), and Gary Becker's (1957) model of discrimination with that of Åsa Rosén (1993). By doing so I will show that the policy implications of Ott's and Rosén's models are feminist, in contrast to the policy implications of Becker's models. Concluding remarks are given in the last section.

NEO-CLASSICAL ECONOMICS AND FEMINISM – SOME DEFINITIONS

Some feminist scholars plead for 'feminist economics' in contrast to 'neo-classical economics', which they view as too limited (cf. Folbre 1994). I do not agree. Usually neo-classical economic theory is considered to start with the marginal utility analysis which was developed around 1870 independently by Stanley Jevons in England, Carl Menger in Austria and Leon Walras in France

(Blaug 1985a). This dating is uncontroversial, but ideas as to what later developments are included or excluded from a definition of neo-classical economics seem to differ considerably between different scholars. One definition of neo-classical theory includes macro-economics until Keynes and micro-economic theory. Another definition excludes recent developments in micro-economics such as bargaining theory, the economics of uncertainty, property rights, etc. However, most authors include the works of Gary Becker and 'Economics of the Family' under the label 'Neo-classical Economic Theory'. I will also include this theory and all other economic theory that accepts price theory and marginal utility analysis. Neo-classical theory in my definition is synonymous with mainstream economics and includes recent developments in micro-economics such as bargaining theory. This includes the models of Ott and Rosén as well as Becker.

We also need a definition of a feminist. It is easy to show that economic theory has been created by men. Blaug (1985b and 1986) has written two books in which he presents 100 famous economists before Keynes and another 100 after Keynes. Only three of these 200 famous economists are women: Rosa Luxemburg, Joan Robinson and Irma Adelman. Only recently have women entered the economics profession. The situation where I work in the Department of Economics of the University of Amsterdam is typical. Of forty-six tenured full professors, only two are women. In my country of origin, Sweden, the only female full professor of economics was appointed in January 1993, although some fifteen to twenty women now hold doctorates in economics in Sweden, the earliest dating from about 1976. In the United States there are more female professors of economics, although they are less likely to be full professors, and only a few are at the ten 'top' universities.

Although women are more likely to be feminists than men, having more women in the profession is no guarantee of having more feminism in the science of economics. There also needs to be gender awareness. One definition of a feminist is 'someone who recognizes the disadvantaged position of women and is willing to do something to change this in personal and professional life' (Kuiper 1993). Obviously many women and some men are feminists according to this definition.

However, wanting to change implies that you know where you want to get to. It is necessary to have a vision of a society which does not favour men to the disadvantage of women. To me the vision is of equal role sharing between men and women. Men should take half the unpaid caring work and women half the paid work, half the incomes, half the power and half the glory (Gustafsson 1991). People are not feminists in my view if they think that children need their mothers all the time; that it is all right for fathers to be almost totally absent from their children's lives and just provide the money; and that women who want careers must forsake having children while men can have both.

Neo-classical economics is about marginal changes in prices and incomes, and it cannot give us a long-term vision. But using the tools of neo-classical economics with a gender awareness can give us arguments for reforms leading to a society which is at the same time more economically efficient and closer to the vision of a feminist. Neo-classical economics is the best theory for analysing changes in prices and incomes, and many policies have effects on prices and incomes in a broad sense, including psychic incomes, as Becker (1964, 1981) and others have taught us. Also prices and incomes have effects on many aspects of human behaviour that previously were not considered, such as marital and divorce rates, fertility rates and time usage. It is therefore extremely important that feminists take part in this work and do not give it up in favour of working on the vision.[2]

DIVISION OF WORK WITHIN THE FAMILY

In this section I will contrast Gary Becker's (1981) model of the division of work within the family to that of Notburga Ott (1992). By using a dynamic perspective, Ott challenges the standard wisdom that specialization in the household brings efficiency gains.

Gary Becker's model of the division of work

Gary Becker's (1981) model of the division of work within the family assumes that a woman and a man start out with the same intelligence and the same education. Division of work within the family will be profitable because of gains from specialization in work and investment. If the couple have a child the woman is biologically more productive in housework and she will increase her advantage in household production the more time she spends in this activity. She is investing in household-related human capital. Very small differences in comparative advantage lead to large differences in behaviour.

In the same way the man will increase his productivity in market work the more time he spends doing market work because he improves his skills and therefore makes on-the-job investments. The household therefore gains from each partner specializing in his or her task and then trading with each other. This theory of marriage has also been called the 'trade model' or the pure transaction model. This model describes an important economic mechanism and it is excellently presented in a textbook by Blau and Ferber (1986). A more formal textbook presentation is offered by Cigno (1991).

The model is illustrated in Figure 3.1. Consider a man (Jim) and a woman (Kathy) who have unequal comparative advantage in household production and market work. The upper panel of the figure shows the production opportunities open to each of them if they perform in isolation, and the lower panel shows the gains from specialization and exchange. If Jim

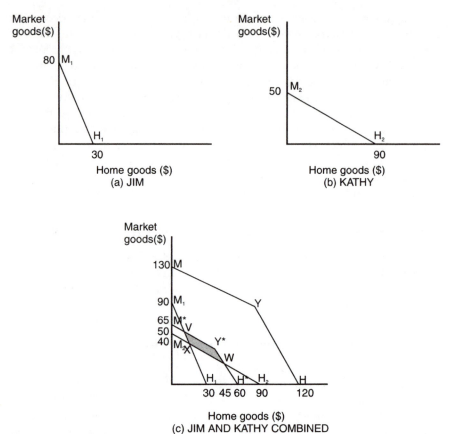

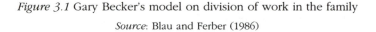

Figure 3.1 Gary Becker's model on division of work in the family

Source: Blau and Ferber (1986)

spends all his available time in market work he can earn $80 and if he spends all his available time in household production he can earn the shadow income of only $30. The shadow income is defined as the purchases you can avoid by household production, e.g. restaurant meals, bread, cleaning services, etc. If Kathy spends all her available time in market work she can earn $50 but if she spends all her available time in household work she can earn $90. In the lower panel the $30 of Jim's potential home goods are added to the $90 of Kathy's potential home goods on the horizontal axis and the $80 of Jim's potential market goods are added to the $50 of Kathy's potential market goods. The combined household can then produce according to the 'production possibility curve' of MYH where YH has the slope of Jim's exchange rate between home production and market production, i.e., his wage, and MY has the slope of Kathy's wage.

The lines M*Y*H* delimit a space which is half of MYH. The shadowed area VY*WX is the efficiency gain as compared to what each could produce as a one-person household. As long as each individual prefers a balanced mix of home goods and market goods, they are better off together than apart. Only if Jim prefers to have almost exclusively market goods at a point above and to the left of V is he better off in a one-person household. Likewise if Kathy prefers almost exclusively home goods, at a point below and to the right of W, she is better off on her own than in the combined household.

Consider a situation where only market goods are produced and both Jim and Kathy work full-time in the labour market at point M. If the couple now want more home goods they can get that by exchanging market time in favour of home goods time. It is certainly more efficient for the one with the higher productivity in home goods, namely Kathy, to decrease her market time along the line MY. The alternative, that Jim should decrease his market time along the line YH, could only cost more market goods and result in fewer home goods being produced. Therefore whichever point on the production frontier MYH the couple chooses, one of the partners will specialize entirely in one of the activities, and it may be that both will specialize, in a complete role-split. The conclusion that follows from Becker's model is that it is better to specialize. From Figure 3.1 it is easy to show Becker's proposition 1: 'In an efficient household at most one member will spend time in both household and market activities. All other members of the household will specialize in either market activities or household activities' (Becker 1981: Chapter 2).

Notburga Ott's model on division of work

Notburga Ott (1992, 1995) analyses the division of work within the family using a bargaining model. Each partner maximizes his or her own utility, and then there is negotiation between them. The model is a co-operative bargaining model with a Nash solution. In the model the threat points are determined as the points of utility that each partner can achieve if the marriage breaks up. If there is a co-operative game the partners can agree, as in Becker's model, that the woman does household work and the man works in the market, and their joint utility will be increased. However, if we make the model dynamic and introduce a second period, the woman's bargaining power will decrease and she will be worse off than if she had not agreed to withdraw from the labour market.

The model is illustrated in Figure 3.2. Let us assume in the first period that the threat points are given by D^f_I and D^m. The threat points in turn are determined by the labour market earnings of each partner. The Pareto efficient solution is delimited by the feasible set D_IOP. The Nash solution (co-operative bargaining model) will be along a 45-degree ray from the origin of the feasible set, so the optimum point is A. In A, the man has a slightly higher utility than the woman.

If the woman agrees to specialize in household production she lowers her threat point due to the loss of market-related human capital investments and/or depreciation of her human capital due to non-use. Her threat point is therefore lower in the second period, as illustrated by D^f_{II} in Figure 3.2. We assume that the man's threat point does not change. The woman's lower threat point gives a new feasible set $D_{II}OR$. The solution to the Nash bargaining problem will now become B. At point B the woman's utility has decreased to U^f_{II} and the man's utility has increased to U^m_{II}.

Ott's model implies that the utility of the woman decreases if her threat point is decreased. Her threat point decreases if she has a lower earnings capacity and that of her husband increases if he has a higher earnings capacity.

The difficulty of measuring utility is a well-known problem. Ott has found an interesting illustration by using data from 1,101 German housewives who answered the question: Who has most power in the family? The alternatives were: 1. Your husband; 2. Both have equal power; and 3. You have most power yourself. It turns out that the wife has more power if she has higher education or an income of her own, i.e. if her threat

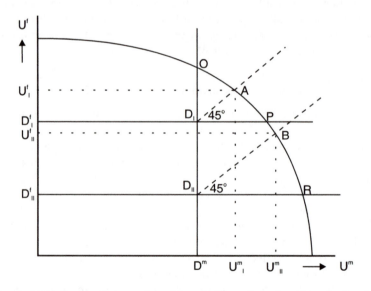

Figure 3.2 Notburga Ott's model of the division of work within the family

Source: Ott (1992)

point is higher. She has less power the higher the husband's income and if there is more housework, i.e., they own a house and the children have not left home. Ott's power regression therefore is in accordance with her theory.

A woman who tries to combine family and career often comes to a point at which her time use and that of her husband are in conflict. The assumption of a joint utility household function has therefore been criticized by feminists. Ott provides us with one of the few examples of alternative economic models and explanations which are more in accordance with women's desire to achieve equality with men in the labour market and in society.

Policy implications

Becker's model is not meant to be normative, yet many feminists have understood it as a policy recommendation in favour of the traditional family. However, it is easy to show, using Figure 3.1 above, that the smaller the difference in comparative advantage, the smaller the wage differential between Jim and Kathy, the smaller the specialization gain will be. If Jim and Kathy earn exactly the same market wage and exactly the same shadow wage in household work there will be no specialization gain. The feminist policy implication that follows from Becker's model is therefore to minimize the wage differential in order to achieve a redistribution of paid and unpaid work between the two. However, according to Becker's model such a policy is likely to be accompanied by an efficiency loss. His model predicts that as wage differentials between men and women narrow there will be less specialization, which is also in accordance with empirical observations over time. However, there is a difference between a 'natural' development towards smaller gender wage differentials and a change induced by policies. The latter is not to be recommended according to Becker's theory because it will decrease the efficiency of the economy.

In Chart 3.1 the crucial differences between Ott's and Becker's models are summarized. Ott focuses on an aspect which is neglected in Becker's model, namely on the possibility that there may be conflicts within an existing marriage. Using Ott's model it can be shown that the German government, implementing policies which it thought would increase fertility, has in fact introduced fertility-decreasing policies. Child and family support in Germany are almost exclusively in the form of tax deductions on the larger of the two incomes of the couple, thereby increasing the bargaining power of, in most cases, the man. A woman will have to choose between having a child and losing bargaining power or having no child. If she chooses to have a child and stays home her situation is comparable to a prisoner's dilemma game. Both partners will gain if they choose to have a child because the utility frontier is then, in Figure 3.2, shifted outwards. He will have an incentive to assure her that her utility will not be decreased if she chooses to have a child, but she has a diminished bargaining position in future renegotiations. Jacob Mincer (1978) coined the term 'tied marriages', in his work on family migration decisions, to denote the situation where one spouse loses as a result of migration but the gain of the other spouse is bigger than the loss of the 'tied mover'. The concept would appear to be applicable here. Thus the policies of the German government are likely to lead both to tied marriages and a suboptimal number of births, according to Ott.

In Becker's model feminist goals can only be achieved at the expense of efficiency unless one assumes that there are other rewards as well as monetary rewards for market work; whereas in Ott's model feminist goals are consistent with improved Pareto optimality in the sense of making both partners better off because they can choose to have a child.[3]

One final point is that Ott's model does not exclude Becker's model. Both economic mechanisms may be present simultaneously and the choice of policies is ultimately left to politicians, who must judge which goals and which economic mechanisms are considered most important.

Chart 3.1 Division of work within the family

BECKER	OTT
Division of work and trade lead to specialization gains	*Division of work* lowers the home-working partner's threat point, leads to tied marriages and fertility decisions as prisoner's dilemmas
Feminist goals can be achieved by trading off efficiency for equity	*Feminist goals* can be achieved by policies which simultaneously improve Pareto optimality i.e. economic efficiency
Policies to promote feminist goals might decrease economic efficiency due to decreased specialization gains	*Policies* to promote feminist goals, e.g. subsidized childcare, paid parental leave and tax rules benefiting the two-earner family, might increase economic efficiency

DISCRIMINATION THEORY

In this section I will contrast Gary Becker's (1957, 1971) model on discrimination to that of Rosén (1993). A vast number of studies in many countries have shown that women are paid less in the labour market than men with the same education, experience and age (See Löfström and Gustafsson 1991, Michael et al. 1989, O'Neill 1985, Schippers 1987). This difference in pay is because women have different jobs to men, and these are lower paid. To pay a lower wage to women than to men for the same job is ruled out by anti-discrimination laws.

Gary Becker's discrimination model

The economic study of discrimination also owes its origin to Gary Becker, whose work on discrimination (1957) precedes his work on human capital (1964) and on the division of work within the family (1981). Becker assumes that there are equally productive men and women, but that the employer discriminates against women and therefore employs women only if they can be paid a lower wage which equals the men's wage minus the discrimination coefficient. The argument is illustrated in Figure 3.3.

Wage discrimination refers to a case in which the discriminated group is paid a wage which is lower than its actual productivity. It is a well established result in economic theory that the wage for a group of workers is set equal to the marginal productivity of the last hired worker. A non-discriminating employer would therefore either employ N_0 workers and pay the corresponding wage at C or employ N_1 workers and pay the corresponding wage at E. However, the actual equilibrium wage will be determined by the interaction of demand with supply, which determines the wage at which a worker wants to supply his or her labour to the market. At a higher wage more workers want to supply their labour than at a lower wage.

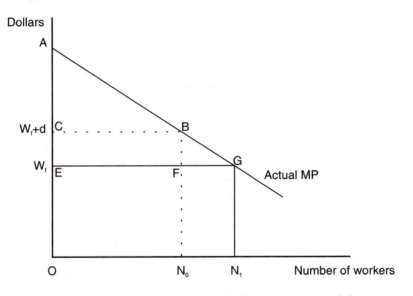

Figure 3.3 Gary Becker's 'taste for discrimination' model

Source: Ehrenberg and Smith (1982)

In Figure 3.3 the actual marginal product is the negatively sloped demand curve for labour ABG. A discriminating employer will employ women only to the point where their marginal product equals the employer's subjective value which is W_f+d.[4] The discriminating employer will therefore employ N_o women and make a profit of AEFB, paying women the wage W_f. A non-discriminating employer however would employ women to the point at which their actual marginal product equals their wage. He or she will employ N_1 women and make a profit of AEG. The discriminating employer pays men at their actual marginal productivity and employs N_o men at the wage $W_m = W_f + d$.

Suppose that only men are employed in the first period. However, if the employer discovers that he or she can get equally productive women workers at the wage W_f, she can make a profit by employing women instead of men. The men will find it increasingly difficult to find employment at their going wage and will start accepting jobs at a lower wage rate, or the women will become a scarce factor of production and will be able to start bidding up their wage. The competition will end discrimination after some time.

Becker (1993), in his Nobel lecture, argues that his theory has been misinterpreted as implying that discrimination will disappear in the long run. His own words in Becker (1971: 45) are:

> It does not necessarily follow from this analysis that the market discrimination coefficient (MDC, which is d/W_F) would be greater than zero. For example if the production functions of each firm were linear and homogeneous, the MDC would equal zero if at least one employer had a zero DC.

The reasoning above, based on Ehrenberg and Smith (1982), of course describes this simple version of Becker's model.

However, according to the reasoning in Becker's own text the non-discriminating employers may not be able to expand their production because of increasing costs with output, i.e. the production functions are not linear and homogeneous, and competition would then not result in vanishing discrimination coefficients among employers. The size of the discriminated group in comparison to the majority group affects the outcome. Becker (1993), in his Nobel lecture, also considers discrimination from customers and fellow-workers to be far more important than employer discrimination, and says that the optimal response, if the employer is non-discriminating and the workers discriminate, is for the employer to segregate men and women into different departments. If there are not enough women with the required range of skills, discrimination against women cannot end by segregation. Further, most feminists also regard segregation as an undesirable outcome.

Åsa Rosén's discrimination model

Åsa Rosén (1993) has developed an alternative model of discrimination, in which the match between jobs and people is essential. Rosén's model starts, just like Becker's model, by assuming that employers discriminate. However, the discrimination mechanism is that women get fewer job offers than men, in contrast to Becker's model in which women are paid less.

In Rosén's model starting salaries are the same for all workers in period 1. In the second period a wage negotiation between the worker and the employer based on the productivity of the job match takes place. This is also different from Becker's model, in which the wage plus the discrimination coefficient clear the market to equalize the probability of getting a job offer. The crucial mechanism of Rosén's model is that different matches between workers and jobs produce different productivities. Thus Rosén's model is a matching model, based on the search theory literature (cf. Pissarides 1990).

Rosén assumes that there is asymmetric information in the labour market. The worker knows his own true productivity for a certain job. But the employer does not know it at the time of the hiring decision. The kind of knowledge that the worker has relates for example to ability to work independently, ambition, capacity to work long hours, ability to co-operate and ability to endure stress. This type of information is typically not available on the curriculum vitae of the person.

The basic ideas of Rosén's model are illustrated in Figure 3.4. There is a probability density function $f(q)$ for any job match between a worker and a job. The per period value (productivity) of a job match is q. For any worker this probability density function over jobs is the same and for any job the probability density function is the same over all workers. However, a match between one worker, e.g. worker W, and one job, e.g. job 1, is different from the match between a different worker, worker M and the same job. If worker W is matched with job 1 the resulting per period productivity will be q^w_1 in graph a and graph c in Figure 3.4. If worker W on the other hand is matched with job 2 the resulting per period value of the match is considerably higher, namely q^w_2, as illustrated in graphs a and d. We can now look at the matches from the point of view of filling the vacancy for job 1 shown in graph c. If the vacancy for job 1 is matched with worker W, the resulting per period productivity will be q^w_1, but if worker M gets job 1 the resulting productivity per period will be q^m_1. Likewise for job 2, shown in panel D, the match between worker M and job 2 will produce q^m_2 and the match between worker W and job 2 will produce q^w_2. It would be most efficient if worker W were matched with job 2 and worker M were matched with job 1. The opposite match will produce a loss of $q^m_1 - q^w_1$ plus $q^w_2 - q^m_2$ for the economy. If there is discrimination and worker W belongs to the group which is discriminated against this is exactly what will happen, as Rosén points out.

47

Rosén assumes that employers discriminate on the basis of a visible index which may be sex or race or blue eyes, by not making as many job offers to members of the discriminated group. The probability of getting a job offer plays a crucial role in the model, because it determines the cut-off rate, or reservation wage, below which a worker searching for a job will not consider applying for the job. If the probability of getting a job offer is smaller for a woman than for a man, the woman's cut-off rate will be lower than the man's. Assuming now the worker W belongs to the discriminated group, in this case women, and worker M to the non-discriminated group, men, this is depicted in Figure 3.4 as the cut-off rates q^w_c and q^m_c respectively. If worker M gets more job offers his cut-off rate is at a higher level, as shown in graph b, namely q^m_c. This means that worker M will not apply for job 1 because it is below his cut-off rate. Worker W will accept job 1, thinking that she will not be offered job 2 because the probability of her getting a job offer is smaller. Because worker W now produces a lower q than worker M since $q^m_2 > q^w_1$, employers will find that they were right in their suspicion that female workers are less productive than male workers. The fact that a different matching would produce a higher overall output is never revealed.

The model predicts that discrimination can persist even in the long run, and the outcome cannot be avoided through entry or segregation. Rosén shows that there is a steady-state equilibrium in which all firms discriminate against the same type of worker, that any stable equilibrium is *necessarily* discriminating and that a worker of the discriminated group will have to score significantly better in order to be hired.

Policy implications

In Chart 3.2 I have summarized the basic differences between Becker's and Rosén's discrimination models. First the basic forces driving the two models, their assumptions about employer behaviour, are different. Becker assumes that employers pay women a lower wage, and that men's and women's probabilities of employment are equal given women's lower wage. Rosén assumes the opposite. She assumes that starting salaries do not adjust downwards for the discriminated group. Instead women get fewer job offers. Becker's discriminating equilibrium is unstable, destroying itself in time under at least some conditions, whereas Rosén's discriminating equilibrium is stable and will not destroy itself. This also means that Rosén's result implies that there is a need for affirmative action in order to achieve the economically more efficient non-discriminatory equilibrium at which the best matches are achieved, i.e. the situation in which q^w_2 and q^m_1 are realized, as in Figure 3.4. However, the values of q^m_1, q^m_2, q^w_1 and q^w_2 may be different from as drawn in Figure 3.4. It may be that there is no non-optimal job matching or that the loss from not having worker W in job 2 is

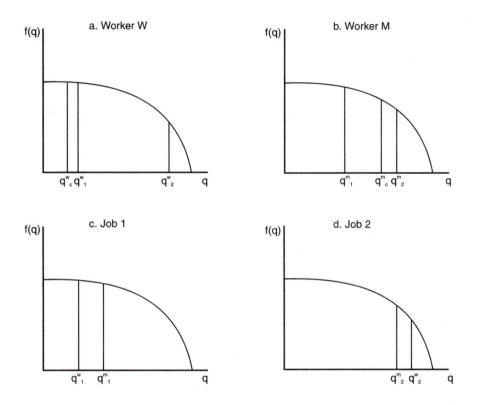

Figure 3.4 Åsa Rosén's matching model of discrimination. Distribution of productivity of job/worker matching

compensated for by a gain from having worker W in job 1, if worker W should happen to be more effective in both jobs.

In Rosén's model only a few firms need to deviate from the non-discriminatory equilibrium for it to be possible for all firms to do so. This is in contrast to Becker's model in which, under some conditions, one non-discriminatory employer could out-compete the discriminatory employers. Rosén's model is consistent with many empirical phenomena, including women's and black's lower wages, higher unemployment and greater likelihood of being in bad jobs. Paying equal wages to all workers within narrowly defined occupations is also not enough to end discrimination. The equal pay policy has not ended discrimination since discrimination is coupled to hiring practices. This is an argument against adding occupation or level of occupation as one of the explanatory variables in an analysis of wage differentials between men and women. It is important to consider hiring practices as a part of discrimination, in addition to the difference in wages.

Chart 3.2 Discrimination

BECKER	ROSÉN
Employers have *a taste for discrimination* and discriminate against women by paying them a lower wage equal to their subjective cost of employing women.	Employers discriminate against women by *not making job offers* which results in women accepting less efficient job matches than men.
Feminist goals of equal wages can under some conditions be achieved *automatically* with time because non-discriminatory employers will make profits and drive discriminating employers out of business.	*Feminist goals* will not materialize without action because *discriminatory equilibria* are the only stable equilibria.
Affirmative action, quotas etc., that do not affect the coefficient of discrimination may result in less productive persons being hired and may decrease efficiency of the economy.	*Affirmative action* will lead to *better matches* and may increase the efficiency of the economy.

CONCLUSIONS

This chapter has shown how two female economists, Ott and Rosén, working within the neo-classical tradition have developed original economic models which are much more in accordance with feminist thinking than previously accepted economic models of the division of work within the family and discrimination. Their work, however, builds on the extension of economic theory into areas that were not analysed and were not possible to analyse by economic methods before the development of the field of the economics of the family, in which one of the most prominent theorists is Gary Becker. Whereas the policy recommendations from Becker's model of the division of work, given that efficiency is desired, are for specialization, the recommendations from Ott's model are against specialization. Similarly the policy recommendation of Becker's discrimination model can be interpreted to be against affirmative action policies, whereas the results of Rosén's model imply that affirmative action policies may improve the efficiency of the economy.

This chapter is an argument for feminist neo-classical economics. By examining two original models developed by female economists which add to the achieved knowledge in the field, I wanted to show that economic theory is likely to change as more feminists enter the profession.

If an economist is convinced that there is no discrimination against women he or she will search for an economic explanation showing there can be no sustainable discrimination in the long run. However, an economist who is convinced that there is discrimination will search for an explanation of its existence and persistence. Those who are against quotas for women and minorities argue that it is decreasing the productivity of the economy. Rosén's model shows the opposite. If bad matching is the reason for the lower productivity of women then quotas for women will increase the productivity of the economy, not decrease it.

Similarly Ott shows that conflicting interests within marriage will result in suboptimal choices if there is specialization. While Becker's model is silent about the division of the specialization gain, Ott shows that the partner specializing in household production will suffer. This is also empirically confirmed by her 'power' regression.

NOTES

1 An earlier version of this paper under the title of 'Women in neo-classical theory' was presented to the conference 'Out of the Margin, Feminist Critiques of Neo-classical Theory', Amsterdam, 2–5 June 1993.
2 All this is not meant to deny people the right to define themselves as feminists if they want to, in the same way as socialists must be allowed to define themselves as socialists. There may be differences in gender awareness and willingness to act. There are also semantic differences in the connotation of the word feminist. In the United States feminist is the positive counterpart to the negative label sexist, whereas in Germany a feminist is a woman who refuses co-operation with men.
3 Having a child would produce more total utility to both partners, resulting in a parallel upward shift of the opportunity set. But the change from D_I to D_{II} of Figure 3.2 would make the woman choosing a child worse off so that the Pareto efficient improvement will not be realised unless a binding contract can be concluded that shifts the new solution along the 45-degree line $D_I A$.
4 'd' can be considered a disutility for the employer.

REFERENCES

Becker, G.S. (1971 2nd ed.) *The Economics of Discrimination*, Chicago: University of Chicago Press.
—— (1964) *Human Capital*, New York: National Bureau of Economic Research.
—— (1981) *A Treatise on the Family*, Cambridge, Mass.: Harvard University Press.
—— (1993) 'The economic way of looking at behavior' (Nobel lecture), *Journal of Political Economy*, 101(3), pp. 385–409.
Blau, F.D. and Ferber, M.A. (1986) *The Economics of Women, Men and Work*, Englewood Cliffs, New Jersey: Prentice Hall.
Blaug, M. (1985a) *Economic Theory in Retrospect*, Cambridge: Cambridge University Press.

—— (1985b) *Great Economists since Keynes. An Introduction to the Lives and Works of One Hundred Modern Economists*, Cambridge: Cambridge University Press.

—— (1986) *Great Economists before Keynes. An Introduction to the Lives and Works of One Hundred Great Economists of the Past*, Cambridge: Cambridge University Press.

Cain, G.G. (1985) 'Welfare economics of policies towards women', *Journal of Labor Economics*, 3(1) part 2, pp. 375–96.

Cigno, A. (1991) *Economics of the Family*, Oxford/New York: Oxford University Press.

Dijk, E. van, and Hoek, M. (1992) 'They went for the title', *Rostra Economica*, Amsterdam: University of Amsterdam.

Ehrenberg, R.G. and Smith, R.S. (1982) *Modern Labor Economics, Theory and Public Policy*, Glenview, Illinois: Scott, Foresman and Company.

Folbre, N. (1994) *Who Pays for the Kids? Gender and the Structures of Constraint*, London/New York: Routledge.

Gustafsson, S. (1984) 'Equal opportunity policies in Sweden', in G. Schmid and R. Weitzel (eds) *Sex Discrimination and Equal Opportunity, The Labour Market and Employment Policy*, Aldershot: Gower Publishing Company.

—— (1991) 'Half the power, half the incomes and half the glory. The use of microeconomic theory in women's emancipation research', *De Economist*, 139(4), pp. 515–29.

Hagenaars, A. and Wunderink-van Veen, S.R. (1990) *Soo Gewonne soo Verteert, Economie van de Huishoudelijke Sector*, Leiden: Stenfert Kroese.

Harding, S. (1993) 'Feminist philosophy of science. The objectivity question', Report of the 'Out of the Margin' conference, Amsterdam.

Killingsworth, M. (1990) *The Economics of Comparable Worth*, Kalamazoo, Michigan: Upjohn Institute for Employment Research.

Kooreman, P. and Kapteyn, A. (1987) 'A disaggregated analysis of the allocation of time within the household', *Journal of Political Economy*, 95(2), pp. 679–94.

Kuiper, E. (1993) mimeo (Dissertation work), Amsterdam: University of Amsterdam.

Layard, R. and Walters, A. (1978) *Micro-economic Theory*, New York: McGraw-Hill.

Löfström, Å. and Gustafsson, S. (1991) 'Policy changes and women's wages in Sweden', *International Review of Comparative Public Policy*, 3, pp. 313–30.

Lundahl, M. and Wadensjö, E. (1984) *Unequal Treatment. A Study in the Neoclassical Theory of Discrimination*, London: Croom Helm.

Michael, R.T., Hartmann, H.I. and O'Farrell, B. (eds) (1989) *Pay Equity. Empirical Inquiries*, Washington D.C.: National Academy Press.

Mincer, J. (1962) 'Labour force participation of married women: a Study of labour supply', in A. Amsden (ed.) (1980), *The Economics of Women and Work*, Harmondsworth: Penguin Books.

—— (1974) *Schooling, Experience and Earnings*, New York: National Bureau of Economic Research.

—— (1978) 'Family migration decisions', *Journal of Political Economy*, 86(5), pp. 749–73.

—— and Polachek, S. (1974) 'Family investments in human capital: the earnings of women', *Journal of Political Economy*, supplement 82, pp. 76–108.

Nelson, J.A. (1992) 'Gender metaphor and the definition of economics', *Economics and Philosophy*, 8(1), pp. 103–25.

O'Neill, J. (1985) 'The trend in the male–female wage gap in the United States', *Journal of Labor Economics*, 3(1) part 2, pp. 91–116.

Ott, N. (1992) *Intrafamily Bargaining and Household Decisions*, Berlin: Springer Verlag.

—— (1995) 'Fertility and division of work in the family', in E. Kuiper and J. Sap (eds) (with S. Feiner, N. Ott and Z. Tzannatos) *Out of the Margin: Feminist Perspectives on Economics*, London/New York: Routledge.

Pissarides, C.A. (1990) *Equilibrium Unemployment Theory*, Oxford: Basil Blackwell.

Rosén, Å. (1993) *An Equilibrium Search, Matching Model of Discrimination*, working paper, no. 102, FIEF, Stockholm: Trade Union Institute for Economic Research.

Schippers, J. (1987) *Beloningsverschillen tussen Mannen en Vrouwen. Een Economische Analyse*, Groningen: Wolters-Noordhoff.

Schultz, Th.W. (ed.) (1974) E*conomics of the Family, Marriage, Children and Human Capital*, National Bureau of Economic Research, Chicago: University of Chicago Press.

4

DISCRIMINATION AGAINST WOMEN: A NEO-INSTITUTIONALIST PERSPECTIVE

Barbara Krug

INTRODUCTION

From a public choice perspective, discrimination, in general terms, describes a specific form of behaviour by one group of economic actors within a particular society *vis-à-vis* another group. A classical example of such discrimination is the behaviour of men *vis-à-vis* women. Clearly many men – though by no means all – have found it advantageous to exclude women from the labour market and public life. Discrimination, however, was not limited to a tacit agreement, or a conspiracy, among male 'chauvinists'. On the contrary, discrimination has been openly displayed and defended on religious or pseudo-biological grounds, and it became institutionalized through laws and regulations. In other words, discrimination was based on collective action by one sector of society which succeeded in imposing an institutional setting that made it possible to allocate income, life chances and upward mobility according to criteria other than individual effort, skill or education. The question which needs to be dealt with today, however, is not how discriminating institutions emerged, but why they could – and can – persist.

As will be shown in what follows, discrimination would vanish in the long run only in situations of perfect competition among societies (or economies) and zero exit costs. But in the absence of these conditions, the abolition of discrimination depends on the interaction between the discriminating and the discriminated groups *within* one society. Our economic analysis here is based on the assumption that, if discrimination exists, there must be a market for it. Positive supply in this market is based on the number of economic actors who have an incentive to discriminate and face only 'soft' constraints which fail to offset this incentive. Positive demand, on the other hand, arises from the fact that some women, at least, have an incentive to accept discrimination. As will be shown, incentives and constraints do not merely reflect preferences or 'natural' differences.

54

Institutions also generate incentives and determine constraints. It is in particular

- the nature of labour and marriage contracts;
- the system of collective bargaining and the internal labour market;
- state-imposed family law and tax legislation; and
- the interdependence among the family, the labour market and the political process

which allow different groups of economic actors to extract economic rents to the detriment of women. The abolition of discrimination, therefore, requires collective action which insists on institutional change rather than demanding compensation payments – or that men change.

TAKING THE LONG VIEW: WHY CAN DISCRIMINATING SOCIETIES SURVIVE?

Assume a society composed of two groups: a discriminating group and a non-discriminating group. Can the two groups co-exist? According to neo-classical analysis (Becker 1957, cf. Gustafsson in this volume) they cannot. The non-discriminating group in which resources, including labour, are used and rewarded according to marginal productivity will generate higher growth rates and higher income, a process further accelerated by scale and scope economies. That society will prove 'fitter' for survival so that in an evolutionary process the discriminating group will be driven out.

But this is not what happens in reality. The discriminating male group has not disappeared. Three factors can be singled out to explain this phenomenon (Frank 1985). First, in order for the non-discriminating group to exploit its comparative advantage, it needs non-discriminating individual actors. In other words, its advantage depends on the likelihood that individuals find a non-discriminating partner for all manner of transactions: as employers, as marriage partners or as trading partners. To this extent sociological or feminist studies are right: the disappearance of discrimination depends on value changes by at least a part of the membership of the dominant group.

Aside from the total number of non-discriminating partners in a society, the geographical distribution of 'dissenters' also plays a role. If, for example, the non-discriminating group is concentrated in the Scandinavian countries while the discriminating group is mainly to be found in Southern Europe, mobility and mobility costs determine the relative weight of each group. Other things being equal, under the condition of zero mobility costs, segregation or secession would take place until all discriminating individuals were concentrated in the south, while all non-discriminating individuals would concentrate in the north.

The third factor, often overlooked in economic analysis, derives from the fact that members of the discriminating group are not easily identified. If all – and only all – males were to discriminate, or if all – and only all – of those with red hair were discriminated against, identification would be simple (and costless). Since this is not the case, resources have to be employed to detect actual behaviour. Thus, the costs of scrutiny determine mobility and subsequently the chance of dealing with like-minded partners. It ought to be kept in mind that the identification problem and the sometimes considerable scrutiny costs enable the discriminating individual to cheat. The incentive is almost irresistible. It is profitable to pretend to be a non-discriminating employer or husband before the contract is signed.

In short, the mobility and scrutiny costs, as well as uncertainty, limit the extent to which there will be clustering according to the two groups' preferences. Such an analysis focuses on exit as the decisive driving force for institutional change. The analysis would predict segregation or secession caused by the migration of people and capital to a sector of society or of the economy in which jobs, investment, property rights or life chances would honour individual contributions to overall income, regardless of sex. This kind of exit does actually occur within the limits stated above.

It should be noted that exit does not refer to migration within and among nation states only, but to departure from the official, male-dominated, economic sector, as well as from mainstream social organizations, such as the traditional family. This trend is to be found in all western industrialized countries where women, regardless of the overall economic situation, drop out of the official labour market. Empirical research has also shown that self-employment, which allows women to avoid organizational discrimination, is also booming and that companies founded by women are by far the fastest growing economic sector in the United States.[1] Similarly, people are increasingly exiting to other life-styles in the form of the rapid growth of cohabitating unmarried couples or single households with a female head.[2]

However, these trends are clearly not powerful enough to initiate institutional change. Despite the improvements, and the rhetoric and lip service, women cannot progress beyond a certain point. But if exit offers only a partial solution, protest might be an alternative. This leads to the further question: how does discrimination work in the short run and, in particular, within the constitutional framework of Europe?

THE SHORT VIEW: THE MARKET FOR DISCRIMINATION

As long as the discriminating and the non-discriminating group co-exist in one society, economic analysis must assume that there is a market for discrimination. This means that there is a positive supply of, and a positive demand for, discrimination, the intersection of the two indicating the amount of discrimination observable and its corresponding 'price'. For public choice theory it is essential to enquire who are the actors on the supply and demand side, how are the two curves constructed and what institutional arrangements co-ordinate demand and supply.

Public choice theory begins with the assumption that discrimination is the outcome of individual decision-making by economic actors who behave rationally in the sense that they compare the expected returns of different courses of action. Consequently, discrimination is supplied as long as the (marginal) costs of doing so do not exceed expected returns, while discrimination is demanded as long as the (marginal) gains exceed the income chances available in non-discriminating ventures. In other words, the shape of the two curves is determined by the marginal costs for discrimination and marginal gains from the acceptance of discrimination.

It is worth considering more closely what determines these gains and costs. As we will see, the relative prices for different courses of action are only partly determined by the specificity of labour markets and individual marriage contracts. Relative prices also reflect the existing institutions. As long as the inherited institutions keep the costs of discrimination low while the costs of combating discrimination are kept high, a reduction in discrimination depends on collective action in the political market. Thus the political process has to be included in the model as an endogenous factor in order to explain the amount of discrimination observable in different countries.

WHO SUPPLIES DISCRIMINATION?

Public choice theory abandons the rather strict assumptions of the Becker (1957) model that discrimination is

- displayed predominantly by employers;
- based on a 'natural' taste;
- unviable in the long run due to competition.

Instead, public choice theory enquires what makes discrimination a profitable venture and why such a course of action is not punished via the price mechanism in working competition. As a starting point, five groups of actors can be singled out: companies and direct superiors, unions, job incumbents, husbands and political parties.

Companies and direct superiors

Unlike the neo-classical entrepreneur, modern companies, in particular worker's direct superiors in the firm's hierarchy, have an incentive to discriminate as long as the (mis)allocation of a female job profile (to a specific job with a lower productivity and corresponding lower wage rate) generates an economic rent. This rent, in the form of less work effort on the part of the superior, or in the form of a larger wage fund at his/her disposal, can be extracted and consumed by the superior directly and personally, while the loss in terms of the misallocation of labour has to be borne by the company as a whole. The leeway for discrimination is made possible by:

- the nature of labour contracts, which necessarily have to be formulated as open, relational contracts allowing *ex post* opportunism (Simon 1957: 183);
- high or increasing firm-specific know-how leading to increasing sunk costs and the chance for employers to 'hold up' a rent if employees face higher sunk costs than the employer when terminating labour contracts (Hashimoto 1981, Hart 1984, Kaye and Aickin 1986);
- the institutions of the internal labour market. Wage rates linked to jobs should – in theory – reflect the distribution of productivity within the overall production process. In reality the definition of jobs or high-end job profiles are the outcome of the collective bargaining between the company (or industry) and the unions.

As empirical studies have proved, misallocation of labour depends a great deal on unspecified job profiles and the invisibility of actual performance (Steinberg 1985: 146–53, Bianchi and Spain 1986: 186). The more specified jobs are, the easier it is for the employee herself or competing employers to assess the productivity level required, and the lower the costs of combating discrimination. Invisibility of actual performance and lack of specificity of job profiles also allow superiors to overlook women when it comes to promotion, and explains the widening of the income differential at higher occupational levels. In other words, leaving 'female' job profiles unspecified leads to the 'crowding effect' (low wage rates for women due to an oversupply of female labour in low productivity work places; see Edgeworth 1922: 431–57)[3] and the kind of job market segregation that can be observed today: women get stuck in low-end, low-income jobs.

In brief, while in standard economic theory the (neo-classical) firm is presented as one which cannot discriminate due to competition in the labour and product market, the theory of the modern company shows that these constraints work only 'softly' when it comes to the internal labour market. Here, asymmetric information, monitoring costs or – in general – the intra-firm incentive structure limit the extent to which the chief executives or owners will force the personnel who allocate labour to forgo discrimination. So far the analysis suggests that discrimination depends on the number of discriminating superiors within one firm or on the incentives to enforce an optimal labour allocation within each company. However, as has already been suggested, the uniformity of behaviour in discriminating industries in Europe is also influenced by the system of collective bargaining which facilitates discrimination as long as unions do not find it profitable to pursue an anti-discrimination policy.

Collective bargaining and unions

Wages are only one parameter in collective bargaining. More decisive for women are the following issues which link a specific job profile, such as 'female', to a specific job.

First, trade unions and employers' associations negotiate over two sets of jobs: those filled from external recruitment and those filled from internal sources, i.e., from the firm's or a government agency's existing stock via promotion. This division arises from the fact that employees recruited from the internal and external labour markets are not regarded as perfect substitutes. The need for on-the-job training partly explains the difference, but there are other causes, as will be seen. The higher the number of positions to be filled from internal sources, the more difficult it becomes for women who have temporarily dropped out of the labour market to recapture a position compatible with their profiles. In other words, the collective bargaining system defines a (re-)entry barrier for labour supply from the external market.

Second, trade unions and employers also define job profiles and job requirements. The level of formal education, intra-firm training schemes and the number of ranks within one occupation all play a part in collective bargaining. To define jobs dominated by a female workforce as unskilled, or low-end jobs which need no further intra-firm training, is a common practice throughout Europe. Thus, for example, a secretary in Germany faces four different ranks, and thus promotion chances, while a metal worker in a car plant can climb upwards through eleven ranks. In other words, actual income chances depend less on the marginal labour product equals wage rate rule, as neo-classical economists assume; instead, administrative rules and customs shape labour contracts. If both partners in the collective bargaining want to discriminate they can do so at low costs.

Third, collective bargaining defines, finally, a 'fictional' standardized work profile, based on male lifetime work. In Europe standard employment refers to an unlimited work contract asking for at least 35 hours of work per week. A widening of this standard to include women and their need for more flexible lifetime work is not costless. We know that group evaluation is the more efficient, the more homogeneous the group is with respect to whatever characteristics are considered important. Thus, adjusting the standardization in order to allow for a more heterogeneous job profile increases information costs and bargaining costs for *all* labour contracts since *each* individual case has to be considered instead of relying on rough indicators.

This shows that the employment of women does not imply higher labour costs due to gender-related fringe benefits only, as is often argued. Rather, labour costs are higher because women's (or other minorities') lifetime job profiles do not accord with the existing standardization of work profiles based on the (assumed) homogeneous group of (white) males. In other words, to end discrimination it is necessary to have unions which fight for this in collective bargaining. This is not what we observe in Europe. Even in Sweden, unions were more than reluctant to do so. The public choice literature can explain this. Unions should be seen as another internal market by which the demand for, and supply of, discrimination is co-ordinated, via majority voting among their members. It has been shown (Frey 1983: 88–101) that union leadership aims at revenue, prestige and bargaining power not by vote or membership maximization but by proposing a policy that secures a comfortable majority. A union leadership cannot gain by taking up women's issues as long as women (or those favouring an anti-discrimination policy) do not add up to a high proportion of total membership.[4] Unions have positive incentives to design policies which satisfy the demands of a majority of their members. This suggests that the unions' weak response to women's demand is determined by the composition of unionized labour. To blame the predominantly male members for discrimination, however, would be misleading, as will be seen in what follows.

Internal labour markets and job incumbents

Regardless of whether they are unionized or not, those who already have jobs have an incentive to favour 'closed shops'. Union membership represents an effective means to do so, with non-members enjoying a free-riding position. Clearly, the incumbents can extract an economic rent by limiting access to the labour market. The exclusion of women is not restricted to their exclusion from occupations, but can also take the form of limiting upward mobility, i.e., restricting access to higher positions within one occupation (Bielby and Baron 1986). By limiting access, the labour supply is artificially reduced (in particular in higher ranks), which in turn causes the wages of incumbents to remain higher than the equilibrium wage rate. The difference in income is an economic rent enjoyed by all incumbents, while the costs in the form of the misallocation of labour are dispersed throughout the whole economy. An econometric study for the United States, for example, shows that white males enjoyed, in the 1980s, an average wage that was 6 per cent higher than it would have been in the absence of discrimination (Cotton 1988: 15–28).

Since not all incumbents are male, women who are seeking access cannot rely on female 'solidarity' or on the altruism of their employed sisters or female trade union leaders. Thus the supply of discrimination does not strictly follow gender lines. But there is one group that is closely linked to gender: husbands.

Family organization and husbands

As the economics of the family has shown, all husbands (or partners in long relationships) face an incentive to 'discriminate'. By doing so they can extract an economic rent in the form of disposable time, i.e., time spent neither on income-earning activities outside the home nor on household chores. The misallocation of household time is one of the most remarkable puzzles for the social sciences: regardless of culture, of the legal or traditional norms employed, regardless of changes in the labour market participation of women and in their market income, household work is not allocated according to relative productivity and wage rates as neo-classical analysis would expect.

Instead, husbands shirk the household chores and, subsequently, enjoy more leisure time and higher wage rates. The latter is called the male marriage premium and is evident in the income differential between married and unmarried male employees.[5] The fact that men can shirk derives from the nature of the formal or informal marriage contract. First, a well-formulated contract, taking into account all contingencies, runs counter to the kind of co-operation envisaged, since only trust and the voluntary forgoing of self-interest ensures the kind of relationship aimed at. Otherwise there would be no difference between a marriage and a business partnership (Boulding 1978: 21–37, Cohen 1987: 267–303). Second, the distribution of the gains from marriage is not legally enforceable during the marriage but only at the time of the break-up (Papps 1986, Cohen 1987). Third, child-bearing implies additional marriage-related, non-transferable investment which leads to higher sunk costs for women than men at the time of the divorce. It is this difference in sunk costs which allows men to bargain for a favourable share of the co-operation rent (Sen 1990: 123–47, Ott 1992).

All this suggests that discrimination in marriage is the result of private and voluntary contracting. However, to conclude that state intervention is unnecessary would be misleading since – as will be shown in what follows – the existing institutions work to the detriment of women.

The political parties

As already indicated in the case of collective bargaining, discrimination is not the result of private contracting alone. It is also influenced by collective action in the past, i.e., the inherited institutions. Thus, for example, the establishment of the modern welfare state generated a spin-off effect that freed women from providing social services within the family. Another example is tax legislation and family law, which define the transaction costs for combining marriage and parenthood with work in the market (Meyer 1987: 22–8, Manser and Brown 1980: 31–44). In other words, the political process in the past as well as in the present generates relative prices for the different courses of action among which women (or men) can choose: to stay single or to get married, to work inside the family or to seek outside employment, to bear children, and so on. The relative prices are set by tax legislation, including social security schemes, by family law (marriage, divorce and custody law), and by labour market regulation (Backhaus 1991: 4–10).

The question which then arises is why, despite a dramatic reduction in time input for household work due to smaller families, household appliances and the creation of the welfare state, and despite an increasing demand from women for lifelong employment; why, despite all this, has there not been a corresponding change in the institutional setting in all European countries? Since institutional change depends on the political market where the demand and supply of institutional change is co-ordinated, the working of the European party systems has to be taken into account.

Here, as public choice theory shows, the same reasoning as in the case of the unions can be applied. Political parties will find it profitable to offer institutional change only if this will affect their election chances or – at least – will not endanger their re-election. They will compare additional votes based on an anti-discrimination policy with expected losses in response to such a policy. Here again the majority rule creates a threshold effect: marginal changes in the number of votes matter only if they occur around the majority winning mark. If all women were to base their support for political parties only on discrimination issues then a corresponding institutional change would have occurred long ago.

To conclude that the continuance of systematic discrimination in a democratic system which allows all women to vote for or against relevant issues 'proves' that a large number of women do not want institutional change is misleading. First, the intensity of the demand is not accounted for and, second, the European electoral systems (with the rare exception of a referendum) do not encourage single-issue voting. Whether anti-discrimination issues will be the decisive factor therefore depends on the policy packages offered by the competing parties and the trade-offs between the different components in the package. Public choice theory in such a situation would suggest that as long as the discrimination problem does not play a major role for the median voter and as long as, consequently, none of the existing parties has an interest in designing a corresponding policy, new parties may emerge which try to capture the votes of those who do concentrate on discrimination issues. However, the leeway that existing parties enjoy, i.e. the rent they can extract, is defined by the liabilities of collective action: high initial costs and the free-rider problem. Nevertheless, new parties which offer an anti-discrimination policy, such as the Green Party in Germany, do often attract a high share of votes from women. In other words, party competition and declining voter support for the two big parties in Germany (the Social Democrats and Christian Democrats) are the factors which made both of these parties embrace part of the policies offered by the Greens.

On the other hand, even within a frame of working (political) competition, the necessary institutional change will not occur if the majority of voters see no benefit in it. As long as different groups of society can extract rents under existing institutions, an economic analysis would expect to find rent-seeking in the form of 'distributional coalitions' which, by influencing the political process, attempt to safeguard the rent-creating institutions. As was shown above, this form of collective action can utilize political parties or unions. In Europe, normally, conservative parties offer a platform for protecting the interests of husbands and modern companies while labour (or social democrat) parties tend to represent the interests of unions and those who already have work.

This sobering view of the supply side of discrimination is not, however, sufficient to explain the amount of discrimination that occurs. A fuller examination must take into account the fact that discrimination would not occur if this supply were not buttressed by a positive *demand* for discrimination.

THE DEMAND FOR DISCRIMINATION

A positive demand for discrimination implies that women accept employment (or marriage) offers despite the fact that they do not get the same pay as their male colleagues or the same share of total household income. Economic analysis assumes in such a case that women accept discrimination if – and as long as – the expected monetary and non-monetary income in the best – non-discriminating – alternative is lower than income in discriminating workplaces (or marriage). If the two sets of alternatives are not perfect substitutes and if we dismiss the interpretation of 'natural' propensities to discriminate or accept discrimination, then other factors must be assumed to be at work. Economic analysis can expose three such factors: transaction costs, family organization and feedback effects.

Transaction costs

Transaction costs here refer to the information costs, search costs and sunk costs which women face when entering the labour and marriage markets or when they consider switching jobs or marriage arrangements.

Information costs and search costs depend on the total number of non-discriminating employers (husbands) and their geographical distribution. The smaller or more dispersed the number of non-discriminating contract partners the higher the search costs. Moreover, since the existing labour and marriage contracts allow for the extraction of economic rents, it is profitable for prospective employers and husbands to promise more than they are willing to fulfil once the contract is concluded. Thus women face high scrutiny costs in finding somebody who will not exploit the possibility of *ex post* opportunism which is embodied in open, relational contracts, such as labour and marriage contracts. In both kinds of contracts women also face higher exit costs than the contract partner, due to the high sunk costs created by contract-specific know-how. In the case of work contracts such sunk costs emerge when they, more than men, work in unspecified jobs without formal training, since intra-firm training is less transferable to other workplaces. Again, the difference in sunk costs for employers and female employees determines the 'holdup' of the rent.

Formal education, on the other hand, is not necessarily a remedy for women. Dropping out of employment for some years, for example, can reduce the value of education: the re-entry chances and wage rates offered then depend on the employers' depreciation rate and the kind of formal education acquired. It can be shown that a degree in the natural sciences faces higher depreciation than a degree in German literature (Weck-Hahnemann 1993). In marriage contracts, higher sunk costs arise from child-bearing and having custody of children, both factors making women less eligible in the marriage market.

All these cost components (information, search and sunk costs) can add up to transaction costs which make any change of workplace or marriage partner costly, and more costly for women than for men.[6] Change is profitable only if the difference in expected life income covers the cost of change. In an extreme case, the costs of change can be so high that a non-discriminating alternative is not taken even if, once concluded, it would offer higher returns or no discrimination.

While the transaction costs have to be reckoned with by all women, married women face additional constraints.

Family organization

Contrary to what is postulated by neo-classical analysis, women's labour force participation rate cannot be explained by wage differentials between a husband's and a wife's market wages and differences in productivity for household work. While the opportunity costs – the wife's market income which is forgone – can explain the increase in labour force participation, a corresponding re-allocation of time for household production cannot be observed (Becker 1965: 493–517). Instead, the need to combine employment with the family causes a change in the labour supply function, which appears as a derived function adjusted for household time. Parenthood, in particular, influences:

- the total working time available, and its distribution over the day and over a lifetime;

- the geographical boundary of the labour market in which employment is sought;
- total working effort (current as well as the willingness to embark on additional training).

At first sight one cannot see why the necessary adjustment should discriminate against women, and all the more so if the analysis is based on the neo-classical model which treats the family as an 'as-if' market in which choices between income sources and the allocation of time follow relative productivity and relative wage rates. Here too, the new approaches to the economics of the family, concentrating on private contracting and bargaining models (Manser and Brown 1980, Pollack 1985: 581–608), provide further insights with respect to the problem of how the gains from marriage (the co-operation rent) are distributed. As these models show, the break-down position or threat point, i.e., the point at which co-operation is ended (divorce), also affects the partners' respective bargaining power during the preceding co-operation (marriage). The break-down position describes the individual welfare position which the two partners can expect if they re-enter the labour market as singles or switch to another marriage partner (Sen 1990, Ott 1992, cf. Gustafsson in this volume).

If women face a lower individual welfare position than men at the time of divorce, then husbands can extract a quasi-rent during the preceding marriage since women will comply with an unfavourable sharing arrangement for the co-operation rent (McCrate 1988: 235–39). In this analysis, the women's demand for discriminating marriage contracts is explained by different exit opportunities (Gustafsson 1992: 61–85). At first sight it does not seem that the difference should necessarily follow a gender line. But, as has already been indicated, women face lower exit opportunities due to higher sunk costs for mothers and the scarcity of non-discriminating employers and husbands. Therefore an economic analysis would not be expected to show that women in general will be exposed to discriminating 'marriage' contracts. Instead, we would expect that couples without children would agree to a fairer sharing rule. Similarly, women living in non-marital relationships, which allow them more exit opportunities, should enjoy a more equal share of the co-operation rent and of the household burden. Empirical studies prove this (Gustafsson 1990) and explain why, for example, the percentage of unmarried couples with children has increased rapidly in the last twenty years in Europe, so that today it is the dominant form of the family in Scandinavia.

To what extent do the different exit opportunities lead to a change in demand for discriminating marriage arrangements? The different exit opportunities for men and women define different welfare positions at the time of divorce. As these models show, the individual welfare positions define the threat point, i.e., the point at which co-operation is ended by a divorce. They also show that the difference in welfare positions affects the partners' respective bargaining power during the preceding marriage. In other words, the lower the welfare position at the time of divorce for women, the lower is the share of the co-operation rent during the preceding marriage which they can claim.

Therefore women could improve their exit opportunities – and subsequently their bargaining position within the marriage – by staying within the labour market and by pursuing an independent career. However, such a course of action is not costless. State legislation creates labour participation costs which are higher for couples with children than for childless couples or singles, and which are higher for mothers than for fathers.

Tax legislation

In most European countries, the tax authorities stop short of the family. Income (in kind) generated by household production is not taxed and therefore adds directly to the overall marriage gain. Therefore, the higher the marginal income tax for (women's) market income, the higher the threshold against re-entering the labour market after marriage (Backhaus 1991, Gustafsson 1990). Similarly, the higher the consumption tax on close substitutes for the goods and services produced in the household, the higher this threshold. Thus the higher the marginal income tax rate for married women and the higher the consumer tax on household substitutes, the lower the labour force participation rate of women will be. This is so because married women base their calculation on after-tax income adjusted for the expenses necessary in order to buy substitutes. A study in the United States, for example, showed that the 35 per cent household income differential caused by the wife's re-entry to the labour market shrank to a mere 17 per cent when the substitution of market for non-market production was taken into account (Kermit 1992).

The influence of taxation is not limited to tax rates, as the following example shows: while in the German system couples are taxed jointly at lower rates than single income earners, in Sweden both husband and wife are treated and taxed as individuals (Schettkat 1987: 37–46). The German system also imposes higher tax rates for the second income earner than for a single person doing the same job. Tax legislation thus generates labour participation costs for married couples with children. Not surprisingly, the labour force participation rate of married women is lower in Germany than in Sweden, reflecting the higher participation costs for second income earners who, in the German case, are mostly women.[7] The question which then arises is why we find that the second income earner is normally female. Here again, in addition to the other factors listed above, state legislation sets incentives.

Family law

Although family law in Europe differs widely between Ireland and Sweden, the effects on women are similar: it affects (life) income and it affects the time budget and hence the income opportunities for women negatively. On the one hand, when the divorce risk increased considerably after the Second World War, a risk to which women reacted with increasing labour force participation, the drop in life income at divorce, on the other hand, has limited exit opportunities and caused women to stay in an unsatisfying relationship. In the terminology of the bargaining model: the lower individual welfare level at the break-down position is also caused by existing family law, in particular by custody law and entitlements to pensions.

A closer look at family law and labour market regulations reveals that the neo-classical analysis of the family (for example in Becker 1981) represents an extreme case in which there is no state legislation. As can be assumed, and as empirical studies have proved, families do not maximize market income but rather after-tax income, and adjust for implicit prices generated by state legislation. The case of Sweden has proved, for example, that granting

- paternal leave for either of the parents (instead of 'maternal' leave);
- entitlements to re-employment after paternal leave; and
- entitlements to build up pension rights during paternal leave

causes a reallocation of work and time within the family in the direction that an economic analysis would predict: a higher labour force participation rate of women throughout their working life and a more equal sharing of the household burden (D'Amico 1987: 14–26).

In countries such as Germany, where the above-mentioned reforms have not been made and in which there is joint taxation, total family income is maximized if one parent stays at home and specializes in household production. Here state legislation generates high transaction costs for both parents if they attempt to combine parenthood and professional work. Depending on relative wages, this system may also create incentives for a complete role-reversal, in which the husband stays at home. However, as long as cases in which women at the time of marriage earn considerably more than their prospective husbands are rare, the existing state legislation enforces the traditional division of labour which enjoins women to stay at home.

All in all, it is state legislation that generates implicit prices to which families respond when allocating work and time. It is also state legislation which (in conservative countries such as Germany) establishes barriers to a more equal sharing of professional and household work between husband and wife. By concentrating on intra-family decision-making, this analysis suggests that the demand for discriminating marriage arrangements would decline if an increasing number of women were to insist on an independent career or on institutional change in state legislation. That not all women behave in such a way can be explained by feedback effects.

Feedback and learning effects

Often overlooked in the analysis of discrimination are feedback effects. When treated at all, the analysis usually follows Becker's study (1981), which proved that parents act rationally when, with a limited budget, they invest less in daughters as long as the expected returns are lower than returns from investment in sons. This explains the perpetuation of discrimination for women over generations. The calculus can also be used to explain the low investment of women in human capital during their lifetime. As long as women know – or learn – that professional training offers low returns, or less than for their male colleagues, they act rationally by dropping out of the career paths (Ferber, Green and Spaeth 1986). This explains the often-heard complaint that women do not seem to want to embark on training schemes.

Political activities are another area in which the same feedback effect works. When women discover the high investment costs of organizing themselves (and the free-rider problem), or when they learn that individual party or union membership offers low returns, they act rationally by keeping aloof from politics. As said before, the net return will remain lower for women than for men as long as female membership stagnates at a low level, and as long as women enjoy less disposable time.

A third kind of feedback effect occurs in the bargaining game between husband and wife. The winner in one round of bargaining gets not only a more favourable outcome but, simultaneously, a better position (bargaining power) in the future. As was pointed out earlier (Gustafsson's chapter in this book), employment outside the family improves the individual break-down position. Likewise, once women agree to the traditional division of labour due to child-bearing, their bargaining position in *all* future rounds of intra-marriage bargaining worsens.

THE LONG VIEW REVISED: WHY CAN DISCRIMINATION SURVIVE?

The analysis has shown why discrimination can survive even if the 'natural' taste to discriminate declines (to zero). As long as the existing institutions offer economic rents which make it profitable for one or several groups in society to discriminate against women, discrimination will be supplied. The supply will meet positive demand depending on income differentials between discriminating and non-discriminating alternatives *and* on the transformation costs of changing the existing institutions. Discrimination in Europe is a rent-seeking activity based on attempts to limit access to economic and political advancement for women. While compensation schemes offer different returns for the same activity according to sex (and marital status), the economic rents created by such schemes do not follow a clear gender line (D'Amico 1987). It would therefore be misleading to blame only 'men' for discrimination. Instead, as the analysis presented here reveals, discrimination is also an institutional problem.

Discrimination occurs under different regimes: in hierarchies (within the internal labour market), under market competition (i.e. the external labour or marriage market), under the majority rule voting procedure, and, finally, in private contracting. It is the latter institution that creates some confusion in economics. Neo-classical analysis assumes that as long as an economic system is based on private and voluntary contracts, there can be no discrimination since women are not forced into specific marriage or labour relations. However, as contract theory proves, this assumption neglects the fact that private (labour or marriage) contracts attempt to secure a steady long-term flow of services (and investment) under numerous contingencies *and* reflect implicit prices (opportunity costs) as set by the institutional framework. As a result, private contracting can generate gender-specific different economic rents. Furthermore, it is systematically more expensive for women than for men to conclude long-term contracts (Sturn and Sturn 1992, FitzRoy and Mueller 1984). It has also been shown that the cost structure within any one segment of the market for discrimination is less significant than the whole bundle of costs from all segments which reinforce each other.[8]

In such a situation, women are left with two alternatives: exit or protest. The analysis has shown why neither exit nor protest (within the internal labour market, the unions or in the political market) will necessarily be successful. Nevertheless, we observe both courses of action: women do leave the official labour and marriage market, and, at the same time, they organize themselves and raise their voices. As was shown recently (Hirschmann 1993), this behaviour might prove successful *if* enough women participate. While exit and protest have been, analytically, regarded as mutually exclusive, in the sense that any increase in exit rates leads to a drop in the effectiveness of women's protest, both alternatives can be mutually reinforcing depending on the level of exit. The more exit the more protest, because increasing exit reduces the total amount of economic rents available, leaving each discriminating actor a smaller share. In order to protect 'total' income, even discriminating actors have an incentive to protest and vote for institutional changes which would bring women back into the official labour and marriage market. To put an end to the exclusion of women from labour markets and high-end jobs would increase overall productivity which could be used for compensating the discriminating actor for a loss in his/her economic rents. In this case, too, the message is that women do not have to wait until men have changed. Destroying the gains from discrimination, i.e., destroying the economic rents is a powerful means of suppressing discrimination.

NOTES

1 The number of female-owned businesses jumped by 57 per cent between 1982 and 1987. During the same period the overall number of businesses grew just by 14 per cent (*International Herald Tribune*, 4 October 1990).

2 In 1993, 16 million Germans lived in one-person households, 60 per cent more than at the beginning of the 1970s. The portion of the younger generation (under 45 years) living 'single' has increased threefold within the last twenty years (quoted from *Saarbrücker Zeitung*, 16/17 January 1993). International comparisons can be found in Bianchi and Spain (1986) and in Ermisch (1990).

3 The crowding effect was detected by Edgeworth. In Bergman's (1986) version women are restricted by *demand* factors to a limited set of occupations in which the capital–labour ratio is relatively low. Thus, women's work *must* reveal a lower productivity than men's (Blau and Jusenius 1976).

4 In Germany, female membership has been stagnant since the middle of the 1980s at around one quarter of the unionized work force. According to the statistics, only the union for white collar and office work within public administration (*Deutsche Angestelltengewerkschaft*) has a female membership of as much as 40 per cent. It is thus no surprise that this union is the only one with a female head.

5 In the United States the premium typically ranges between 20 and 30 per cent. One study shows that the productivity augmentation of married men is dependent on their wives' time input. It is worth emphasizing that cohabitating men also earn a premium (Kermit 1992). For Great Britain the estimates are not much different. A study shows that being married affects male earnings favourably by up to 5.8 per cent, and female earnings unfavourably by up to 4 per cent (Miller 1987).

6 An empirical test is provided in Madden (1987).

7 See Gustafsson (1990). The United States also has joint taxation. An overview of the different tax rates according to marital status can be found in Bergmann (1986: 219).

8 An analysis of discrimination ought to take into account 'entitlement mapping'. In the polemics of Sen: 'The attempt of utilitarianism (neo-classical analysis) to "mute" discrimination by concentrating on the metrics of desire fulfilment (as measured by individual utility maximisation under constraint) creates an "embarrassment". It cannot "wash away" the fact that underfed, underclothed, or over-worked persons exist, and are deeply deprived – no matter what the individual utility metrics say.' See Sen (1990: 128).

REFERENCES

Backhaus, J. (1991) 'The economic taxation of women and the tax system', *Journal of Economic Studies*, 18(5/6), pp. 4–10.

Becker, G.S. (1957) *The Economics of Discrimination*, Chicago: University of Chicago Press.

—— (1965) 'A theory of the allocation of time', *Economic Journal*, 75(299), pp. 493–517.

—— (1981) *A Treatise on the Family*, Cambridge, Mass.: Harvard University Press.

Bergmann, B.R. (1986) *The Economic Emergence of Women*, New York: Basic Books.

Bianchi, S.M. and Spain, D. (1986) *American Women in Transition*, New York: Russell Sage Foundation.

Bielby, W.T. and Baron, J.N. (1986) 'Sex segregation within occupations', *American Economic Review*, 76(2), Papers and Proceedings, pp. 43–7.

Blau, F.D. and Jusenius, C.L. (1976) 'Economists' approaches to sex segregation in the labour market', in M. Blexall and B. Reagan (eds) *Women and the Workplace*, Chicago: University of Chicago Press.

Boulding, K.E. (1978) 'Réciprocité et change: l'individu et la famille dans la société', in A. Michel (ed.) *Les Femmes dans la Société*, Paris: Presses Universitaires de France.

Cohen, L. (1987) 'Marriage, divorce, and quasi-rents; or "I gave him the best years of my life"', *Journal of Legal Studies*, 16(2), pp. 267–303.

Cotton, J. (1988) 'Discrimination and favoritism in the U.S. labour market: the cost to a wage earner of being female and black and the benefit of being male and white', *American Journal of Economics and Sociology*, 47(1), pp. 15–28.

D'Amico, Th. F. (1987) 'The conceit of labor market discrimination', *American Economic Review*, 77(2), Papers and Proceedings, pp. 310–15.

Edgeworth, J. (1922) 'Equal pay to men and women', *Economic Journal*, 32(127), pp. 431–57.

Ermisch, J. (1990) 'Demographic aspects of the growing number of lone-parent families', in OECD, *Lone-Parent Families*, Social Policy Studies 8, Paris: OECD.

Ferber, M.A., Green, C.A. and Spaeth, J.L. (1986) 'Work, power and earnings of women and men', *American Economic Review*, 76(2), Papers and Proceedings, pp. 53–6.

FitzRoy, F.R. and Mueller, D.C. (1984) 'Cooperation and conflict in contractual organizations', *Quarterly Review of Economics and Business*, 24(4), pp. 24–49.

Frank, R.H. (1985) *Choosing the Right Pond*, New York: Oxford University Press.

Frey, B.S. (1983) *Democratic Economic Policy*, Oxford: Martin Robertson.

Gustafsson, S. (1990) 'Labour force participation and earnings of lone parents', in OECD, *Lone-Parent Families*, Social Policy Studies, No. 8, Paris: OECD.

—— (1992) 'Separate taxation and married women's labour supply', *Journal of Population Economics*, 5(1), pp. 61–85.

Hart, R.A. (1984) *The Economics of Non-Wage Labour Contracts*, London: Allen & Unwin.

Hashimoto, M. (1981) 'Firm-specific human capital as a shared investment', *American Economic Review*, 71(3), pp. 475–82.

Hirschmann, A. (1993) 'Exit, voice, and the fate of the German Democratic Republic', *World Politics*, 45(2), pp. 173–202.

Kaye, D.H. and Aickin, M. (1986) *Statistical Methods in Discrimination Litigation*, New York: Marcel Denker.

Kermit, D. (1992) *Does Marriage Make Men More Productive?* Chicago: NORC University of Chicago, Discussion paper 92–2.

McCrate, E. (1988) 'Gender difference: the role of endogenous preferences and collective action', *American Economic Review*, 78(2), Papers and Proceedings, pp. 235–39.

Madden, J.F. (1987), 'Gender difference in the cost of displacement', *American Economic Review*, 77(2), Papers and Proceedings, pp. 246–52.

Manser, M. and Brown, M. (1980) 'Marriage and household decision-making', *International Economic Review*, 21(1), pp. 31–44.

Meyer, W. (1987) 'Was leistet die oekonomische Analyse der Familie?', *Schriften des Vereins für Socialpolitik*, Neue Folge 164, pp. 11–46.

Miller, P.W. (1987) 'The wage effect of the occupational segregation of women in Britain', *Economic Journal*, 97(4), pp. 885–96.

OECD (1990) *Lone-Parent Families*, Social Policy Studies, No. 8, Paris: OECD.

Ott, N. (1992) *Intrafamily Bargaining and Household Decisions*, Berlin: Springer Verlag.

Papps, I. (1986) *For Love or Money?* London: Institute of Economic Affairs.

Pollack, R.A. (1985) 'A transaction cost approach to families and households', *Journal of Economic Literature*, 23(2), pp. 581–608.

Schettkat, R. (1987) *Erwebsbeteiligung und Politik. Theoretische und empirische Analysen von Determinanten und Dynamik des Arbeitsangebots in Schweden und der Bundesrepublik Deutschland*, Wissenschaftszentrum, Berlin: Sigma Rainer Bohn Verlag.

Sen, A. (1990) 'Gender and cooperative conflict', in I. Tinker (ed.) *Persistent Inequalities*, Oxford: Oxford University Press.

Simon, H. (1957) *Administrative Behaviour*, New York: Macmillan.

Steinberg, A. (1985) 'Frauenlöhne: Die Formen der Diskriminierung sind vielfältig', in Arbeitskreis Frauenfrage des IMSF (ed.) *Emanzipation in der Krise*, Frankfurt a. M.

Sturn, D. and Sturn, R. (1992) 'Diskriminierung als Kontraktproblem', *Kyklos*, 45(4), pp. 483–500.

Weck-Hahnemann, H. (1993) 'Krankenpfleger oder Ingeneurin. Die Berufswahl von Frauen und Männern aus oekonomischer Sicht', in G. Groezinger, R. Schubert and J. Backhaus (eds) *Jenseits von Diskriminierung*, Marburg: Metropolis.

Part II

ECONOMIC POSITION OF WOMEN AND MEN

5

ATYPICAL LABOUR MARKET RELATIONS IN THE EUROPEAN UNION

*Danièle Meulders, Olivier Plasman
and Robert Plasman*

INTRODUCTION

In all countries of the European Union (EU), a significant proportion of women participate in the labour market in 'atypical' labour relations, such as part-time employment, temporary employment, unusual schedule employment, self-employment and subcontracting relations. Often, this type of employment involves lower primary and secondary labour conditions. It may also imply more flexibility, for employer and/or for employee.

In this chapter, we concentrate on two forms of atypical labour relations: part-time employment and temporary employment. First, we present the evolution of these two principal forms of atypical employment in the European member states, revealing both common trends and national divergencies. Subsequently, we concentrate on the common trend, tracing the cause of the growth in part-time and temporary work to the general quest for flexibility on the part of both employers and employees. The next section deals with national particularities. The extent of atypical employment may be related to the level of female participation, for example, or to the level of unemployment. The lack of comparable statistical figures, however, seriously limits the possibilities for meaningfully testing hypotheses. Finally, some conclusions are presented.

FACTS AND FIGURES

Before presenting figures on part-time employment and temporary employment, some definitions are required. Of course, many legal or statistical definitions are possible. In the Eurostat Labour Force Survey – our main source – the distinction between full-time and part-time work is made on the basis of the spontaneous answer given by the person interviewed (Eurostat 1992: 45). In the earlier surveys, however, three exceptions are made, concerning:

75

- Greece, where the criterion is whether the number of hours worked is below the number specified in the collective agreement;
- Italy, where the number of hours worked must be below what is customary in the relevant field of employment;
- the Netherlands, where a self-employed or family worker must be engaged in his or her principal activity for less than 35 hours, and an employee for less than 31 hours or for less than 35 hours if this period of activity is considered to be below par (Eurostat 1988: 57).

For temporary employment, the Eurostat definition is as follows:

> A job may be regarded as temporary if it is understood by both the employer and the employee that the termination of the job is determined by objective conditions such as reaching a certain date, completion of an assignment or the return of an employee who has been temporarily replaced. In the case of a work contract of limited duration the condition for its termination is generally mentioned in the contract.
>
> (Eurostat 1992: 45)

This category includes:

- seasonal workers;
- persons recruited by an employment agency and hired out to a third party for the fulfilment of an assignment (unless there is a written contract of employment of unlimited duration with the agency);
- workers with specific training contracts.

Table 5.1 presents data on the levels of part-time and temporary work in the European Union, within the limits of the figures available. There appear to be important differences between the countries. The Northern countries (Denmark, the Netherlands and the United Kingdom) show the highest prevalence of part-time work. Southern countries such as Greece, Italy, Spain and Portugal, and also Luxembourg and Ireland, have low figures for part-time work. Germany, France and Belgium are somewhere in the middle. With respect to temporary work, the picture is somewhat different. Spain has the highest figure; Luxembourg, Belgium, Italy and the United Kingdom have the lowest. It should be noted that part-time employment is essentially female: in 1993 women held between 61 per cent (Greece) and 92 per cent (Luxembourg) of the part-time jobs. Temporary employment is less typically female than part-time employment, although it is generally more frequent for women than for men. Its main characteristic is that it is concentrated in the younger age groups (Meulders et al. 1994).

Since Table 5.1 gives data for the period 1983–93, it is possible to study the growth of part-time and temporary work over a period of ten years. The picture seems rather diverse. With regard to part-time work, some countries

Table 5.1 Evolution of part-time and temporary employment, 1983–93

Country	Part-time employment[a]				Temporary employment[b]			
	1983	1985	1990	1993	1983	1985	1990	1993
Belgium	8.1	8.6	10.9	12.8	5.4	5.7	5.3	4.2
Denmark	23.8	24.3	23.3	23.3	–	12.3	10.7	9.5
Federal Republic of Germany	12.6	12.8	15.2	15.1	–	9.8	10.3	9.1
Greece	6.5	5.3	4.1	4.3	–	–	16.6	5.5
Spain	–	–	4.9	6.6	–	–	29.8	23.6
France	9.7	10.9	11.9	13.9	3.3	4.7	10.4	9.2
Ireland	6.7	6.5	8.1	10.8	6.2	7.4	8.4	7.2
Italy	4.6	5.3	4.9	5.4	6.6	4.8	5.2	4.3
Luxembourg	6.7	7.2	6.9	7.3	2.6	3.9	2.7	2.4
The Netherlands	21.2	22.2	31.8	35.0	5.6	7.5	7.4	8.8
Portugal	–	–	6.0	7.4	–	–	15.8	7.1
United Kingdom	19.0	21.2	21.7	23.4	5.4	7.0	5.2	4.9

[a] Persons working part-time as percentage of all persons in employment
[b] Persons with a temporary job as percentage of all persons in employment

Source: Eurostat, Labour Force Survey, several years (partly unpublished data)

registered a clear increase (Belgium, France, The Netherlands, United Kingdom), whereas in other countries (Denmark, Greece, Italy, Luxembourg) the level of part-time work remained more or less the same. When comparing the different countries, countries with very low levels of part-time work do not seem to have tended towards the level of the others. Of the countries with a level of part-time work higher than 20 per cent in the mid-1980s, only Denmark showed no increase; among the countries with a low level (less than 8 per cent) the frequency of part-time work remained more or less the same in Greece, Luxembourg and Italy. So there is no 'catching-up' phenomenon for countries with a low level at the beginning of the period. On the contrary, it seems that the divide between Southern European countries and Northern ones (from which Ireland and Luxembourg must be excluded) is becoming wider.

With regard to temporary employment, Table 5.1 shows that between 1983 and 1985 temporary employment diminished only in Italy and increased, to varying degrees, in all the other countries. With the exception of Belgium and Italy, the level of growth in temporary work is higher than the growth in part-time work. After 1985, the extent of temporary work decreased in Denmark, Belgium, Luxembourg and the United Kingdom. The frequency of temporary contracts in the other countries showed a more fluctuating pattern, with an increase during the second half of the 1980s and a decrease during the early 1990s. Only the Netherlands registered an increase of temporary employment between 1990–3. The large drop in temporary employment in Greece and Portugal between 1990–3 is rather remarkable, and may be due to a change in statistics. To summarize: although there are some converging trends in the level of temporary employment, they do not lead toward homogeneity in the situations of the European member states.

EXPLAINING THE GENERAL TRENDS

It is interesting to try to discover the factors behind these common trends and national divergencies. What explains the general rise in part-time and temporary work, and which factors can be held responsible for the marked differences which still exist in this respect? Concentrating in this section on the general trends, it is obvious that an important factor behind the growth in part-time and temporary work is the general quest for flexibility and cost reductions.

Part-time employment generally involves a cost advantage for employers, as part-timers often receive a lower level of remuneration than their full-time colleagues (OECD 1992: 27). Moreover, 'part-timers work harder and have a lower rate of absenteeism' (ibid.). Lower corporate costs may also result from legal provisions. In Ireland, for example, the introduction of part-time employment not exceeding 18 hours per week is particularly advantageous for firms, since it exempts them from social security contributions. With minor variations, the same holds for all other countries. If part-time employment is also flexitime employment, the advantages for employers can be synthesized into numerical and wage flexibility (cf. Fèvre 1991). A part-time 'mobile labour reserve' permits the smooth adjustment of the volume of work to fluctuations in productivity (numerical flexibility). In addition, companies avoid the need for overtime (wage flexibility).

With regard to temporary work, Michon and Ramaux (1992) suggest that costs, time and labour control are the three dimensions of the motivation behind the use of fixed-term contracts, from the perspective of the employer. The costs include lower direct labour costs due to the non-payment of seniority bonuses, and the higher training, selection and management costs of using temporary labour. This latter item diminishes the savings realized. But, thanks to the possibility of switching smoothly from an actual to a desired labour force, what motivates firms is less a matter of immediate costs than of avoiding potential ones. The time dimension of their motivation refers to the desire for a better match between hours paid and hours actually worked. In discussing labour control, Michon and Ramaux refer to three practices, namely selection at the recruitment stage, production incentives and the monitoring of individual output. The use of temporary employment for probationary purposes is becoming more widespread. But it may have negative effects on productivity, first, because of the period required for a worker's training and adaptation, and second, because the precariousness of the worker's situation may result in less personal investment on his or her part. But the opposite may also occur, with the hope of a permanent contract and the more intensive monitoring acting as an incentive.

The advantages offered to employers by certain forms of part-time and temporary work are rather obvious. But what impels an individual to work part-time? On the supply side, the possibility of reconciling work and family life is often given as the main advantage of part-time work; part-time work implies the possibility of adjusting working hours to the need to be at home during certain hours of the day or certain days a week. Plantenga (1994), for example, describing the situation in the Netherlands, emphasizes the positive aspect of (long-term) part-time employment as it offers the possibility of an uninterrupted professional career. In addition, the emblematic picture of the 'perfect employee', devoid of all domestic worries – a phenomenon indicative of a rigid social role division – is becoming obsolete. Many women cannot and will not follow this model and there are more and more men who do not see themselves as 'perfect employees' either. In such cases, a part-time job is a rational and positive choice as it breaks away from the classical concept of the 'pure' wage earner.

However, two objections can be raised to the view that part-time employment is a rational and positive choice of suppliers of labour seeking flexibility. These objections particularly apply to low-quality part-time work. First, as long as this part-time activity remains specific to certain categories of workers, as long as it is associated with adverse employment conditions (wages, qualifications and working hours), and as long as its female aspect remains the direct consequence of a rigid separation of roles, one can doubt the existence of any real choice. For many workers, this choice may be the result of a mechanism similar to the one put forward by Bourdieu (1979) in his analysis of educational choices, i.e. the internalization of objective possibilities. Second, one of the features of part-time work is often the flexibility of the working hours involved – in other words, variable or even split schedules corresponding to peak attendance periods that are relatively incompatible with family life. This is particularly the case in commerce and transport.

The Labour Force Survey throws some light on the question of whether the growth of part-time work should be seen as the result of supply or demand factors. This survey gives the proportion of part-timers who are working part-time because they have been unable to find full-time employment. Table 5.2 contains details for 1993. Some tendencies emerge from a scrutiny of this table, namely:

- The majority of part-time workers seem to be satisfied with this type of labour relation. The exception is Irish male part-timers, a majority of whom would prefer to work full-time. This would seem to imply that

Table 5.2 Non-voluntary part-time and temporary employment, 1993

	Non-voluntary part-time employment[a]		Non-voluntary temporary employment[b]	
	males	*females*	*males*	*females*
Belgium	41.2	27.9	35.0	51.0
Denmark	12.0	18.8	41.3	55.6
Federal Republic of Germany	7.7	6.7	–	–
Greece	48.4	31.3	77.2	68.8
Spain	13.7	14.9	86.6	85.5
France	44.2	32.9	–	–
Ireland	54.3	25.6	68.4	55.6
Italy	39.6	30.6	50.7	49.8
Luxembourg	–	–	–	–
The Netherlands	7.7	4.2	44.4	41.0
Portugal	15.3	23.4	79.9	80.0
United Kingdom	28.7	10.5	50.8	37.0

[a] Persons working part-time because they could not find a full-time job, as percentage of all persons working part-time

[b] Persons with a temporary job because they could not find a permanent job, as percentage of all persons with a temporary job

Source: Eurostat, Labour Force Survey 1993

part-time employment is a positive choice. However, one can still wonder whether some rationalization is involved.

- More male part-time workers are involuntarily working part-time than female part-timers. Apparently, it is still the case that more women than men are willing to reduce working hours because of other tasks.
- In two countries – Germany and the Netherlands – the percentages are noticeably low. In these Northern countries, part-time work is more likely to be 'high quality' than in the other countries.

Whereas the (dis)advantages of a part-time position are not so obvious that all discussion becomes superfluous, the disadvantages of temporary work clearly tip the balance in the negative. Most temporary employees prove to have been recruited either among the unemployed or among those in danger of becoming so, with the expiry of temporary contracts being the most widespread reason for job loss (Michon and Ramaux 1992: 3). The vast majority of workers on fixed-term contracts are in this position because they have been unable to find permanent employment (see Table 5.2). These workers hope to gain permanency when their fixed-term contracts expire. A study for the Netherlands shows that in fact the turnover is rather large; more than 56 per cent of those with fixed-term or flexible contracts in May 1985 had obtained permanent employment by October 1986; some 7 per cent had been unemployed in the interim period and about 37 per cent were still in fixed-term employment (cf. Plantenga 1991). One may conclude therefore that the hard core of those on fixed-term or flexible contracts was probably relatively small, and that the number of transitions is considerable. This also explains why young people's share in temporary employment is so high.

EXPLAINING NATIONAL DIVERGENCIES

With the general quest for flexibility (by employee and employer) explaining the general trend, it remains to ask what factors explain the differences between countries. Although there has been little research, several hypotheses might be formulated to explain these divergencies.

The service sector comprises sub-sectors such as commerce, the hotel and catering industry and health care, in which the phenomenon of 'rush hours' is important. These sectors therefore have a strong need for greater flexibility, which is made easier by the use of part-time or temporary contracts. These sectors also happen to be strongly female and so able to capitalize on the kinds of flexibility typical of female employment. So we will assume that there is a positive relation between the share of the tertiary sector in total employment and the incidence of the two forms of atypical employment.

As women are largely over-represented among atypical employment, we also assume that the higher the level of female participation in the labour market the higher will be the prevalence of part-time and temporary work.

One might expect there to be some relation between the incidence of part-time employment and temporary employment, and the business cycle. According to the 'reserve army' hypothesis, the demand for part-timers is a means of accessing otherwise unavailable female workers in a period of labour shortage. However, Robinson suggests that 'part-time jobs exist in their own right and are not to be regarded as fractions of full-time employees in short supply' (quoted in Morris 1991: 77). Our hypothesis goes in the other direction. We assume that in periods of recession, part-time work can be a cheap way for employers to deal with fluctuating and uncontrollable demand for products and services. In the same way, work contracts for a fixed period have the advantage of flexibility, matching the appropriate volume of work to that required by the demand for products or services. The idea of a link between the growing importance of these two atypical forms of work and a period of recession is thus based on the demand for atypical work.

Finally, we hypothesize that the average wage level will be an important element in the supply of part-time work, with part-time work being more prevalent in countries with higher wage levels. However, it is important to underline the other components of the specific wage relations in a country, such as rates of union membership and the extent of state arbitration of labour conflicts. These aspects should all be taken into account in understanding the different national evolutions of atypical forms of employment.

In order to test these hypotheses, Table 5.3 presents data for 1993 on the level of unemployment, the level of female participation, the importance of the tertiary sector and the average wage level.

The coefficient of correlation between unemployment and part-time employment proved to be very low (see Appendix 5.1). We have to bear in mind, however, that comparing part-time employment with the unemployment rate for only one year and for only twelve countries is a rather simple procedure, and it is impossible to make definitive conclusions on the cyclical or structural character of differences in part-time employment on the basis of this analysis only. The adaptation of supply and demand to the movement of the economic cycle is not obvious. More up-to-date research might reveal more information on the sensitivity of the prevalence of part-time employment to fluctuations in the unemployment rate. Compared to part-time work, levels of temporary work are much more sensitive to the unemployment rate. The coefficient of correlation between unemployment and temporary employment is higher: 0.81. However, this figure is strongly determined by the situation of Spain, which combines a high level of unemployment with a high level of temporary employment. If Spain is excluded, the correlation coefficient drops to 0.33.

When we compare the level of female participation in general with the prevalence of part-time employment, we notice wide differences between countries. High female participation is combined with a low level of part-time employment in Portugal for example, whilst the opposite situation is observed in Denmark. The coefficient of correlation between the level of female activity and the level of part-time employment, however, is not negligible: a value of 0.66. Temporary work is less typically female than part-time employment. Not surprisingly, therefore, there proved to be no relation between the level of female participation on the labour market and the extent of temporary employment (see Appendix 5.1).

Part-time employment is often concentrated in the service sector. In the countries of Northern Europe, this sector accounts for 20 to 75 per cent of part-time employment (Meulders et al. 1994). The increase in part-time employment runs parallel with the growth of the service sector. Yet, the correlation between tertiary employment and temporary employment was proved to be negative (see Appendix 5.1). So, no link can be established between the extent of tertiary employment and the incidence of these forms of atypical work.

With respect to the relationship between part-time work and the wage level, the similarities in the country ranking for the two variables suggest a link between the wage level and the level of part-time employment. This relationship is not automatic: a lower level of part-time employment does not always correspond to a lower wage level. The two countries for which

Table 5.3 Some explanatory variables for the level of part-time and temporary
employment

	Unemployment rate, 1993	Female activity rate, 1993	Share of tertiary employment, 1993	Average wage level (ECU), 1991
Belgium	8.8	39.6	67.9	27,991
Denmark	12.0	61.9	68.8	24,930
Federal Republic of Germany	8.3	47.6	57.8	26,655
Greece	9.4	34.5	54.5	11,150
Spain	28.6	33.8	59.0	20,303
France	12.8	47.7	67.0	26,573
Ireland	18.4	38.6	59.7	20,774
Italy	11.5	33.6	59.6	26,204
Luxembourg	2.4	37.6	70.4	27,148
The Netherlands	6.7	46.6	71.8	26,569
Portugal	5.6	49.5	55.6	8,966
United Kingdom	11.5	52.5	68.6	20,840

Sources: Eurostat, Labour Force Survey 1993; Eurostat, National Accounts ESA, aggregates 1970–91

the wage level is less than ECU 12,000, however, have levels of part-time employment below 8 per cent. Two countries, Luxembourg and Italy, completely contradict this relationship: they combine high average wages and low levels of part-time employment. The coefficients of correlation calculated do not enable us to conclude the existence of a very strong link: the coefficient obtained is 0.38.

These results lead us to maintain the hypothesis of a relationship between the wage level and the level of part-time employment. Of course, the wage level alone does not explain the variations in the level of part-time employment in the member states: other factors such as the level of female participation also influence the development of part-time employment. This could explain the situation of Luxembourg: a low level of part-time employment, a high wage level, but a low level of female participation. On the other hand, the wage level factor enables us to explain the paradoxical situation of Portugal, combining a low level of part-time employment with a high level of female participation. The explanation for the coexistence of a low level of part-time employment and a high wage level in Italy is more complicated. One element may be the development of an underground economy. At a more general level, one could conclude that in countries with a low wage level, part-time employment represents neither an attractive solution for the labour force nor a modality of flexibility preferred by companies. Comparable statistics on the cost of labour would enable us to test the hypothesis of a link between the cost of labour and the modality of flexibility in labour management.

Summarizing our findings, we hypothesize a 'wage level' effect and a 'female activity rate' effect on part-time employment. The level of temporary employment seems to be independent of these factors; no link emerged. With respect to the impact of the economic cycle, we hypothesize that temporary work is sensitive to the economic trend. The increase in part-time employment was also favoured by the employment crisis of the early 1980s, but then it became a structural element in wage relations in Northern Europe. In Southern Europe, however, the region where part-time employment is little developed, part-time employment may be a phenomenon more related to the economic cycle. More research should shed some light on these issues.

CONCLUSION

The two main forms of atypical employment studied here, part-time and temporary work, are linked with particular segments of the labour market. Female employment in the tertiary sector forms the core of part-time employment, and the younger age groups are most important for temporary employment. Both forms of atypical employment increased in the 1980s, especially in the first part of the decade.

Part-time employment is more prevalent in Northern Europe (with the exception of Luxembourg and Ireland) than in Southern Europe. The unequal geographic distribution of part-time employment is partially explained if one takes the level of participation of women in the labour market and the wage levels into consideration. But in relation to the latter factor, it must be said that the lack of the necessary statistics prevents us from drawing more reliable conclusions on the relationship between, on the one hand, wages and part-time employment, and, on the other, the cost of manpower and the level of part-time employment. The geographical distribution of temporary work is difficult to explain. Further research should reveal whether this form of atypical employment is sensitive to the economic business cycle.

Appendix 5.1 Correlation coefficients of the degree of part-time and temporary employment with other rates, as indicated

	N	*Correlation*
Part-time employment and unemployment rate	12	−0.18
Temporary employment and unemployment rate	12	0.81
Part-time employment and female participation rate	12	0.66
Temporary employment and female participation rate	12	−0.06
Part-time employment and tertiary sector employment rate	12	0.68
Temporary employment and tertiary sector employment rate	12	−0.22
Part-time employment and average wage level	12	0.38

REFERENCES

Bourdieu, P. (1979) *La Reproduction*, Paris: Ed. de Minuit. Coll. Le Sens Commun.

Eurostat (1988) *Labour Force Survey, Methods and Definitions*, Luxembourg: Office for Official Publications of the European Communities.

—— (1992) *Labour Force Survey, Methods and Definitions, 1992 series*, Luxembourg: Office for Official Publications of the European Communities.

Fèvre, R. (1991) 'Emerging "alternatives" to fulltime and permanent employment', in Ph. Brown and R. Scase (eds) *Poor Work: Disadvantage and the Division of Labour*, Philadelphia: Open University Press.

Meulders, D., Plasman, O. and Plasman, R. (1994) *Atypical Employment in the EC*, Aldershot: Dartmouth.

Michon, F. and Ramaux, C. (1992) 'L'emploi temporaire, bilan d'une décénnie', *Séminaire d'Economie du Travail*.

Morris, L. (1991) 'Women's poor work', in Ph. Brown and R. Scase (eds) *Poor Work: Disadvantage and the Division of Labour*, Philadelphia: Open University Press.

OECD (1992) *Women and the Restructuring of Employment: Part-time Employment*, Paris: OECD.

Plantenga, J. (1991) *The Position of Women on the Dutch Labour Market, 1983–1989*, Equal Opportunities Unit, DG V, Brussels: Commission of the European Communities.

—— (1994) 'Le phénomène du travail à temps partiel: faits, toile de fond et conséquences', in R. Plasman (ed.) *Les Femmes d'Europe sur le Marché du Travail*, Paris: L'Harmattan.

6

EUROPEAN CONSTANTS AND NATIONAL PARTICULARITIES: THE POSITION OF WOMEN IN THE EU LABOUR MARKET

Janneke Plantenga

INTRODUCTION

One of the most striking developments on the European labour market is the growing activity rate of women. Women have taken up most of the new jobs created in the European Union and have demonstrated an increasing commitment to the labour market, particularly over the core child-rearing years. This does not mean, however, that women have won occupational equality. The concentration of female employment in specific sectors has not changed, and women throughout Europe remain significantly less well paid than men.

Whereas this persistent gender inequality has been the subject of many studies, much less attention is being paid to differences between national states in this respect. The focus is mainly on differences between men and women, overlooking the differences in the socio-economic position of women between countries. These differences are important, however, as they indicate that inequality comes in many (national) colours. Countries may be similar in being gendered, but they are different in the way they are gendered. Focusing on the differences between countries is particularly important from a policy point of view, as the implicit message is that politics do matter.

This chapter provides an overview of the position of women on the EU labour market, in order to extract from it both European constants and national particularities. The chapter is structured as follows. The first part deals with the facts, and presents data on activity rates, occupational segregation and income inequality. The following section is more theoretical and concentrates on the factors behind the differences and similarities in the labour market position of women in Europe. The last section deals with future developments and tries to answer the question of whether some degree of convergence is likely to occur.

An international comparison imposes certain requirements on the statistical material. Here we have made use especially of Eurostat statistics, as the information in these statistics is based on harmonized definitions. This also means that the word 'Europe' and 'European' is used in a rather limited way: in the present chapter we are concerned mainly with a comparison between the (twelve) countries of the European Union.

FACTS: THE POSITION OF WOMEN ON THE EU LABOUR MARKET

On a general level, the 1980s have witnessed the confirmation and the strengthening of trends already seen in the 1970s, namely the steady rise in women's activity rates and the slow decline of male activity rates. These developments have resulted in what has been called the feminization of the labour force, or, in more analytical terms, the growing share of women in the labour force. Table 6.1 gives some data in this respect. In the United Kingdom, for example, the share of women in the labour force has risen from 38.3 per cent in 1975 to 43.7 per cent in 1993. The Netherlands also shows a remarkable increase: in eighteen years the share of women has risen from 24.2 per cent to 40.6 per cent. This feminization of the labour force is the combined result of different developments. On the one hand there is a drop in the activity rates of young people (due to increased schooling) and a drop in the activity rates of elderly people (due to the rise in early retirement). This holds for men as well as for women. At the same time, in the case of women, this decline has been more than offset by the growing activity rates in the age groups between 25 and 49.

Table 6.1 Share of women in total labour force by EU member state, 1975–93

	1975	1985	1993
Belgium	32.5	37.8	41.2
Denmark	39.2	45.7	46.9
(West) Germany	36.5	39.7	42.5
Greece	–	35.4	37.0
Spain	–	–	33.6
France	37.8	42.7	45.0
Ireland	26.3	31.4	36.5
Italy	27.0	34.4	36.7
Luxembourg	28.2	34.9	36.1
The Netherlands	24.2	34.9	40.6
Portugal	–	–	44.7
United Kingdom	38.3	41.4	43.7
Eur 9	34.8	–	–
Eur 10	–	39.3	–
Eur 12	–	–	41.5

Source: Eurostat, Labour Force Survey, 1975, 1985, 1993

The changing labour market behaviour of women can be illustrated using the participation profiles of Figure 6.1. This figure gives the data for the twelve European member states, comparing – if data is available – the situation in 1975 with the situation of 1993. In addition, for 1993 the participation profile of men is included to give some insight into the still remaining inequality between men and women. It should be noticed that 'activity rate' is defined as the number of women (men) in a particular age group actively engaged on the labour market, divided by the total number of women (men) in that particular age group. Figure 6.1 shows that in all EU countries the activity rate of women has risen sharply, especially in the age groups between 25 and 49 years. Large differences remain, however, both between men and women and between women in the different EU countries. In Denmark, for example, participation hardly declines with age, while in Luxembourg and Spain falling participation in higher age groups can be observed. Actually, four typical curves can be distinguished, each reflecting a different participation pattern, namely a single left-hand peak, a bimodal or M-shaped curve, a bell or inverted U-curve and a flat curve (see Plantenga 1995).

The *single left-hand peak* is the typical outcome of a situation in which the two-phase participation pattern still plays an important role in women's labour market behaviour. In this pattern of participation, women work in paid employment until marriage or the arrival of their first child, after which they become full-time spouses, housewives and mothers. This pattern of behaviour is thus characterized by a high level of participation in the younger age groups and a low level of participation in the higher age groups. Ireland and Spain both have a single left-hand peak.

The *bimodal or M-shaped curve* is typical for countries in which the three-phase pattern is common. In this pattern, after the initial period of paid employment, the woman leaves the labour market to devote herself to the birth and care of her children, and resumes working when the children are older. This pattern is characterized by a clear dip in the level of participation around the age of 25 to 35, the so-called child trough. Within the European Union, this M-shaped activity curve is most clearly shown by the United Kingdom.

The *bell or inverted U-curve* comes closest to reflecting men's participation patterns, and is the typical outcome where women's link with the labour market continues through the family phase. However, this so-called 'parallel' participation pattern is often realized by adjusting working hours to the home situation, or by using certain leave facilities. As a result the activity rate may drop quite significantly when a recalculation is made in full-time equivalents. Within the European Union, Denmark comes closest to this pattern.

The *flat curve*, finally, is typical for countries that still have a large agricultural sector. In the agricultural sector, civil status is not an important decisive factor in the labour force participation of women: young girls work after school hours on the family farm, and will continue to do so after marriage. A lot of agricultural work, however, is not counted as such in labour market statistics, so that the labour market participation of women in these countries is rather low; the activity curve of Greece is typical for a country with a large agricultural sector.

Persistent inequality

The increasing participation of European women in the labour market might be expected to lead to equality and integration, breaking down the old boundaries between and within occupations. Evidence suggests, however, that such an expectation is unjustified. The integration of women into men's occupations proves to be a laborious process and women are still strongly overrepresented in the service and clerical occupations and strongly underrepresented in the industrial occupations; see Table 6.2 for further details. From the table it appears that there are strong similarities in the structure of occupational segregation by gender between countries. These similarities are evident in the low female representation among managers, craft workers and plant operators, and women's high shares in services and clerical occupations. There is also some evidence of convergence in some occupational areas. For example clerical work seems likely to move from being a mixed to a predominantly female occupation in all member states, whereas at the beginning of the 1980s the majority of clerical workers were clearly male in some Southern countries and in the Benelux countries (Rubery and Fagan 1993: 6). However, there are also marked differences between countries. As Table 6.2 makes clear, the proportions of professionals (ISCO 2) who are women vary from 29.4 per cent in Luxembourg to 53.7 in Italy, and women's share of employment in the clerical sector (ISCO 4), despite the general increase, still ranges from 49.9 per cent in Italy to 74.3 per cent in the United Kingdom. Women's shares in agricultural and related employment (ISCO 6) show marked differences too, ranging from 7.1 per cent in Ireland to 50.4 per cent in Portugal.

This specific mixture of similarity and difference is confirmed by a European study on occupational segregation, published in 1993. After describing the general tendencies, the writers conclude that: 'Despite the broadly similar pattern of occupational segregation, there are sufficient differences between countries to suggest that social, cultural and labour market forces within each country play an important role in shaping the form and degree of segregation' (Rubery and Fagan 1993: 1). The report also makes it clear that there is no simple relationship between the extent of segregation and the extent of female participation. Women's increasing share in professional employment, for instance, is at least in part associated with women increasing their share of some previously male-dominated

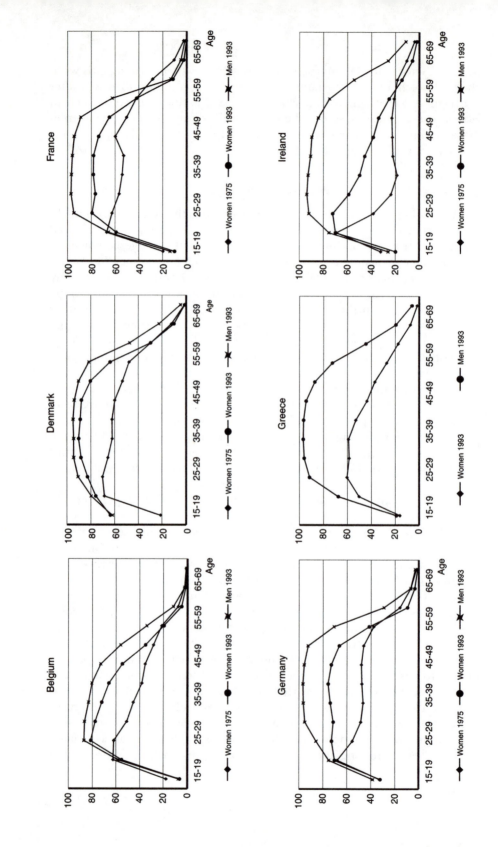

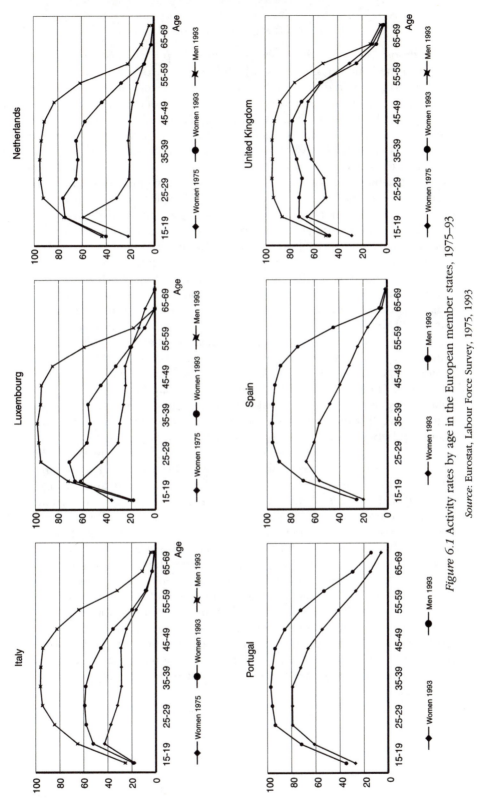

Figure 6.1 Activity rates by age in the European member states, 1975–93

Source: Eurostat, Labour Force Survey, 1975, 1993

occupations. However, the share of women in professional jobs is often higher in the Southern countries, which have lower overall rates of female participation, than in the Northern countries. Moreover it is in the latter that the very high rates of feminization of lower-level occupations are found. Denmark and the United Kingdom, with the highest participation rates of all the member states, display as great a degree of segregation by gender as countries such as Greece or Spain with lower participation rates (ibid.: 9).

One of the consequences of horizontal segregation is that it provides the means by which employers can continue to pay women different wages despite the existence of equal pay laws. The principle of equal pay for work of equal value has not by and large been implemented in the European Union, and pay differentials within and between organizations are still likely to reflect the gendered nature of the employment structure (see also de Bruijn in this volume). In fact, women's pay rose sharply relative to men's in the 1970s in many countries, but in the 1980s the rate of advance slowed and in some cases moved into reverse, despite the continuing increase in female participation and employment rates (Women in Europe 1992: 52). Table 6.3 brings together some of the rather incomplete European data on the earnings of men and women for 1989. It shows that the relative wages of female workers vary from 52.6 per cent for women working in credit institutions in the United Kingdom to 80.8 per cent for female manual workers in France. It should be borne in mind that Table 6.3 is based on data relating only to persons in full-time employment. As women work part-time or have flexible contracts to a far larger extent than men, the actual wage gap between men and women may be even larger.

When it comes to national particularities, the situation in the United Kingdom stands out as especially worrisome. Women doing non-manual work in industry or working in the service sectors earn only about 52 to 55 per cent of the wages of their male colleagues. The situation in Germany seems more positive: especially for non-manual workers and for workers in the service sector, the wage gap is comparatively small. This particular situation also proves that a high level of participation is no guarantee of a narrow pay gap. The United Kingdom has a higher female participation rate than Germany, but its equal pay record is considerably less favourable.

To summarize, one could say that women in the EU member states show remarkable similarities in increasing labour market participation (although it is still less than men), in being overrepresented in clerical and service sector work, and in earning less than men. At the same time there are national particularities with regard to the specific participation pattern, the degree of feminization by sector and the extent of the pay gap. Inequality seems to be a national affair.

Table 6.2 Share of occupational sectors in women's employment and women's share in employment by occupational sector (ISCO-88 (COM)), 1993

	1 Legislators/ Managers	2 Professionals	3 Technicians	4 Clerks	5 Service workers	6 Agricultural workers	7 Craft workers	8 Plant operators	9 Elementary workers	0 Armed Forces	Total
				Share of occupational sectors in women's employment							
Belgium	7.5	23.8	8.3	24.7	15.7	2.0	3.7	3.3	10.8	–	100
Denmark	3.6	10.3	20.7	19.9	24.8	1.2	1.5	4.4	13.5	–	100
(West) Germany	3.7	9.1	24.6	21.2	18.3	1.6	4.7	3.1	13.7	(0.3)	100
Greece	6.5	13.5	5.6	15.8	15.5	24.8	8.7	1.8	7.5	–	100
Spain	7.9	13.4	5.3	18.0	19.7	6.9	4.8	4.2	20.0	–	100
France	1.1	10.9	18.2	24.9	21.5	4.3	2.8	5.6	10.5	0.2	100
Ireland	5.9	21.5	3.0	26.9	25.5	1.8	6.3	2.5	5.6	(1.1)	100
Italy	0.5	14.6	12.8	20.7	20.7	4.6	9.7	4.8	11.5	–	100
Luxembourg	7.7	9.0	11.5	27.8	17.7	(2.1)	(1.7)	(1.6)	20.9	–	100
The Netherlands	5.1	16.1	21.6	20.0	22.7	2.1	1.4	2.6	8.4	–	100
Portugal	6.7	7.3	13.2	14.0	19.2	10.2	13.3	2.6	13.3	–	100
United Kingdom	11.0	14.9	8.0	27.9	21.2	0.4	3.1	3.3	10.2	(0.1)	100
				Women's share in employment, by occupational sector							
Belgium	30.0	53.6	35.2	58.5	65.2	29.1	9.4	16.9	49.1	–	40.0
Denmark	19.3	41.1	56.1	73.1	78.4	28.6	5.9	25.1	50.6	–	46.7
(West) Germany	25.9	35.2	56.3	67.0	74.5	28.8	10.2	16.5	49.7	–	41.7
Greece	22.8	43.9	39.9	52.6	48.8	41.8	16.9	9.1	45.6	(9.8)	35.0
Spain	33.8	48.5	30.1	51.0	51.0	27.0	8.9	12.9	47.5	–	33.6
France	24.7	35.4	49.0	77.0	69.6	33.3	8.8	21.7	60.4	7.1	44.0
Ireland	25.0	51.7	25.5	68.9	54.6	7.1	19.4	10.4	24.5	(16.0)	36.5
Italy	15.1	53.7	33.4	49.9	45.9	32.0	15.5	18.1	39.4	–	34.9
Luxembourg	31.3	29.4	38.9	54.8	64.7	(25.0)	(3.6)	(6.7)	63.2	–	35.8
The Netherlands	17.1	38.3	47.2	65.4	67.3	36.1	5.1	13.2	49.8	–	40.0
Portugal	32.4	49.8	51.3	58.7	60.1	50.4	27.3	17.8	56.2	–	44.2
United Kingdom	34.3	45.0	44.2	74.3	71.2	13.5	10.8	17.6	51.5	(4.6)	45.0

Source: Eurostat, Labour Force Survey 1993

Table 6.3 Gross earnings of women as a percentage of gross earnings of men in six European countries, 1989

	Belgium	Germany	France[a]	Luxembourg[a]	Netherlands[a]	United Kingdom
Gross hourly earnings, female manual workers in industry (NACE 1–5), as per cent of gross hourly earnings paid to men	75.1	73.4	80.8	63.2	75.9	68.8
Gross monthly earnings, female non-manual workers in industry (NACE 1–5), as per cent of gross monthly earnings paid to men	64.5	66.5	64.9	55.6	64.5	55.2
idem, employed in wholesale and retail distribution	62.6	65.8	n.a.	57.1	59.7	55.2
idem, employed in credit institutions	78.4	76.7	65.2	68.6	60.6	52.6
idem, employed in insurance (excl. social ins.)	75.4	78.4	70.0	65.6	67.2	52.6

[a] data for 1988

Source: Eurostat, Earnings – Industry and Services 1 – 1990

THEORY: UNDERSTANDING DIFFERENCES AND SIMILARITIES

While this specific mixture of European constants and national particularities is relatively simple to establish, it is more difficult to explain. Which factors should be deemed responsible for the persistent inequalities between men and women? No doubt there are several, depending on the various dimensions of inequality, but here we will concentrate on a very important one: the unequal distribution of unpaid work. Women as wives, mothers and daughters are expected to be available for unpaid caring work, and are therefore more vulnerable in the labour market. The lower activity rates of women, the large number of women filling part-time jobs and their unequal pay all point to gender-specific social assumptions about the responsibility for providing care.

Although comparative research on the distribution of paid and unpaid work is rather scarce, some information is given by Juster and Stafford (1991). They show the allocation of time for representative samples of men and women in six industrialized countries. Their data indicate that the differences in the total working week between men and women are comparatively small. The extremes are in the United States, where the average working week of men is 3.4 hours longer than that of women, and in Hungary, where the average working week of women is 5.2 hours longer than the working week of Hungarian men. Women, however, spend far more hours doing housework, whereas men spend far more hours doing market work. Interestingly, there appear to be rather small differences in household time among women. They range from 27.0 hours per week in the USSR to 33.8 hours per week in Hungary. For men the differences are much larger, in a range from 3.5 hours in Japan, which is strikingly lower than any other country, to 18.1 hours in Sweden which is substantially higher than the rest (Juster and Stafford 1991: 474–6).

This favourable Swedish record should not be valued too positively, however. Time budget research in 1991 shows that even in Sweden there are still large differences in the nature of time use: women spend a larger part of their time on unpaid labour especially when there are small children in the household. Figure 6.2 gives some information in this respect. The figure shows that for men, the proportion of their time devoted to paid labour hardly changes if they have children – in fact they spend relatively more time on paid labour when there are children under seven in the household. In contrast, women with small children devote just 11 per cent of their time to paid labour, compared to 20 per cent for women without children. The data of Juster, Stafford and the Swedish Statistical Office illustrate the specific participation pattern of men, which has remained relatively unchanged for decades. Because most men leave the care of child and home to their partner, male labour market participation in the 25 to 35 age group does not decrease, nor is the weekly work time adjusted.

This persistent gendered division of unpaid work is also one of the central themes in the sociological research on working couples. Hochschild in *The Second Shift. Working Parents and the Revolution at Home* (1989) clearly shows the pressure which is put on the lives of men and women because of the reluctance of men to take part in household duties. Hochschild describes different strategies men and women use to survive this pressure and to save their marriages. Women are 'supermomming', or cutting back their hours or commitments at work. Others cut back their hours at home, by redefining what the house, the marriage and sometimes what the child needs. As one women puts it: 'I do my half, I do half of his half, and the rest doesn't get done' (Hochschild 1989: 259). Hochschild also shows that many women do not press their husbands to help more. Although they really need more help, they first and foremost want to diminish the marital tensions. Others play experts at home, edging their husbands out, and then collecting credits for doing it all.

Men have different strategies to resist the pressure to share the responsibility at home. Some use the strategy of 'needs reduction'. Hochschild:

> They claimed they didn't need the bed made, didn't need a cooked meal, or didn't need a vacation planned. Indeed, some men seemed to

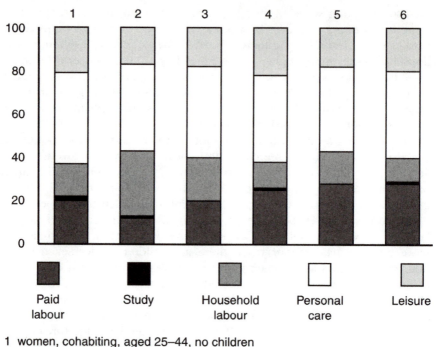

1 women, cohabiting, aged 25–44, no children
2 women, cohabiting, with children under 7
3 women, cohabiting, youngest child aged 7 or more
4 men, cohabiting, aged 25–44, no children
5 men, cohabiting, with children under 7
6 men, cohabiting, youngest child aged 7 or more

Figure 6.2 Time allocation by family phase, Sweden 1991

Source: Statistika Centralbyran (1992)

overtly compete with their wives, over who could care the least about how the house looked, how the meal tasted and what the guest would think.

(ibid.: 260)

Others simply ignore the extra work their wives do at home or try to 'compensate' their not-sharing at home by offering extra money. Still others obscure their strategies by explaining simply that they were not brought up to do the work at home. With these strategies they counterbalance the pressure to participate in household activities and try to save their gender identity, which is already threatened by the fact that their wives work outside the home. And because of this vulnerable male gender identity, women fail to achieve a more just division of unpaid (and paid) work.

This empiric study also shows the limits of an analysis of the division of household time à la Becker. Becker, in short, states that in a two-person household the person with the lowest market income (comparatively) will specialize in household activities. In real life however, things are more complicated, and decisions are not only influenced by economic rationality, but also by gender identities and relating power structures. Hochschild shows that – despite Becker – a more equal distribution of unpaid work is most likely in situations where the man earns at least as much as, or more than, the woman does. In that case his gender identity is not threatened. If, however, she earns more, he wants to be compensated for his loss of power and appeals to his manliness. To quote Hochschild: 'The more severely a man's identity is financially threatened – by his wife's higher salary for example – the less he can afford to threaten it further by doing "women's work" at home' (ibid.: 221).

Inequality as a national affair

So much for the European constants. Now, how about the national particularities? What factors explain the differences in the labour market positions of women, despite the fact that all women are held responsible for the unpaid work? Amazingly little research has been done so far to answer this question. This may be because of the lack of 'a theory of female employment'. There is some general understanding that the differences are related to differences in economic, sociological and demographic factors, yet the complexity of the interaction between these factors makes theorizing difficult. Very often, the labour market position of women in a certain country is explained in terms of its own national history, as the outcome of a highly specific process for which no general laws can be formulated.

During recent years, however, some interesting attempts have been made to go beyond this rather casuistic level. In this new approach the labour market position of women is related to the specific nature of the welfare state. Welfare states are not just a collection of laws and institutions, but are based on and contribute to norms and values of women's (and men's) proper roles. Assumptions about the difference or equality of men and women are more or less institutionalized in the wage structure, the system of social security and the way in which care of the elderly, children and the sick is organized. The specific nature of the welfare state therefore plays an important role in the division of paid and unpaid work and the boundaries between the private and public sphere.

This discussion gained a lot from the work of Esping-Andersen, whose book *The Three Worlds of Welfare Capitalism* was published in 1990. Welfare states, according to Esping-Andersen, are not merely variations of more or less around a common denominator, but cluster around certain principles, of which issues of social stratification, employment and decommodification (described as the degree to which people are independent of pure market forces) are the most important. He identifies three types of welfare states or, as he puts it, three different welfare state regimes: the liberal, the conservative/corporatistic and the social democratic. Yet his book does not elaborate on the position of women. Differences in the socio-economic position of women are mentioned a few times, but the treatment of the subject remains sketchy and fragmented. The main problem seems to be that his notion of decommodification focuses entirely on the relationship between the market and the state, thereby ignoring the interrelationships between the market, the state and the family (Lewis 1992, O'Connor 1993, Orloff 1993, Sainsbury 1994).

Using the work of Esping-Andersen, but taking a more feminist point of view, we can describe the *social democratic welfare state regime* as one which promotes equality at the highest standards among its citizens and is genuinely committed to a full-employment guarantee for men and women. Therefore the costs of familyhood are largely socialized. An extensive system of public services such as childcare, and care for the sick and elderly, ensures that all who are able to participate in the labour market do in fact participate. In other words, the parallel participation pattern is favoured. A basic presumption of the social democratic welfare state regime is that men and women are equivalent. However, this does not necessarily mean that the outcomes are equal. Although the wage differences are relatively small, the labour market is highly segregated along gender lines, as women work largely in public services. In addition, the fact that women do most of the (remaining) unpaid labour is not challenged. There are however efforts to make the combination of paid and unpaid work for women less difficult (Borchorst 1994, Lewis and Åström 1992, Siim 1991). Within the European Union, Denmark comes nearest to this particular welfare state regime.

Within the *conservative/corporatistic welfare state regime*, the family plays a very important role as the anchor of social stability and individual happiness. In contrast with the social democratic welfare state, this welfare state regime is not so much an employer as a (financial) compensator. The conservative/corporatistic regime provides financial compensation whenever the outcomes of the market are deemed unacceptable or workforce participation is considered undesirable. This role as compensator reveals itself in an elaborate system of breadwinner facilities within the tax and social security system. Also in contrast to the social democratic welfare state regime, the conservative/corporatistic welfare state regime does not treat men and women as equivalent. Whereas men are seen as workers, women are primarily seen as wives and mothers, resulting in two different kinds of citizens: men as breadwinners and women as carers. Thus the two-phase participation pattern is favoured. And because the emphasis is on the preservation of traditional familyhood, and not on labour force participation, childcare and/or parental leave facilities are underdeveloped. Within the European Union, Germany, Italy and the Netherlands come nearest to this kind of welfare state regime.

In the *liberal welfare state regime* there is a great belief in the blessings of the market and its self-regulating capacity. The state only functions as a saviour in the last resort: entitlement rules are strict and often associated with stigma. Whereas one can say that the social democratic welfare state regime treats men and women as equivalent, and the conservative/corporatistic regime treats them as different, the liberal welfare state regime treats men and women as equals, disregarding any differences in care responsibilities. A working mother therefore does not really exist in this regime, and the necessity of childcare or parental leave facilities are more or less denied. Of course this influences the labour market position of women greatly. Because this regime has only a limited system of breadwinner facilities, the labour force participation of women is rather high, but the conditions are rather unfavourable. So we would expect a large pay gap between men and women. This particular welfare state regime applies in particular to the United States; within the European Union, the United Kingdom probably comes nearest.

In addition to the three welfare state regimes distinguished by Esping-Andersen, a fourth regime should be mentioned within Europe: *the rudimentary welfare state regime* (Langan and Ostner 1991). In this regime the decommodification effects of the welfare state are still rather modest. States with this regime are typically characterized by a traditional social infrastructure in which the church plays an important role. In addition, they tend to have a relatively large agricultural sector and a rather large informal economy. Care is largely organized on a family basis and is performed by women without payment. Within this rudimentary welfare state regime, women also work in the agricultural sector (mostly as family workers), in the informal sector and in small industries. In other words the participation pattern is mainly agricultural, with its typical flat profile. Within the European Union this regime applies mostly to Greece.

Of course, one has to bear in mind that this typology is only a theoretical construct. No existing welfare state will completely correspond to the ideal picture; all will to some extent be 'hybrids'. Also, much of the complex interaction between the particular welfare state regime and the specific position of women is still unclear and remains to be investigated. Yet, an important advantage of this typology is that it helps to structure a complex reality. It also emphasizes that the 'national particularities' with regard to women are part of a larger whole, which explains why the socio-economic position of women is so difficult to change: it is not only a question of changing attitudes, or providing a few more facilities, but of the socio-economic system as a whole.

FUTURE DEVELOPMENTS

So far, the analysis of women's labour market positions has painted a picture of European constants and national particularities. The remaining question concerns future developments. Is it likely that the inequalities between men and women, concerning wages, jobs and job security will diminish in the near future? And is it likely that the national particularities will dissolve in a process of convergence?

With regard to the European constants, which we translated in terms of the unequal distribution of unpaid work, experience so far is rather disappointing. It should be borne in mind, however, that the reluctance of men to take part in household duties not only refers to the micro level and (failing) negotiations between men and women at the kitchen table. It also refers to the macro level and the necessity to develop a new institutional and social framework that reflects the changed labour force profile and supports equal choices of men and women. This new framework is described most eloquently in the OECD report 'Shaping structural change. The role of women'. This report argues in favour of a movement away from the full-time employment model and the development of a new 'worker profile', described by Passchier (1992) most evocatively as a worker with a 'backpack'. This worker differs from his former colleagues by the fact that he no longer has someone else to take care of home and heart, but combines work with care on an individual basis. Important preconditions are: flexible hours without changing jobs, intermediate part-time work with the option of returning to full-time hours, flexitime, job sharing and the ability to 'capitalize' time over the working week (OECD 1994: 21). Such a fundamental change in existing relations requires a powerful offensive which emphasizes the major importance of these changes. Above all, a cultural reorientation seems necessary. As long as care is described as a burden of unfairly distributed, inconvenient labour, the situation is not likely to change very rapidly. An actual redistribution of paid and unpaid work will only be attainable if care, like paid labour, is seen not as a matter of necessity and duty, but as an essential and enriching part of human life.

With regard to the national particularities, which we translated in terms of the different welfare state regimes, some convergence seems likely. The conservative/corporatistic welfare state regime seems under a lot of pressure. Its assumptions that the family is its smallest unit, and the denial of women's right to work, no longer fit in an increasingly individualized world, in which women (and men) are well educated, in which the right to self-development is hardly contested any more, and in which the pressure to participate in the formal economy is growing. In addition, the financial foundation of this type of welfare state regime seems threatened by continuing internationalization. Agreements made under the terms of the European economic and monetary unification do not forbid breadwinners' facilities, but the move towards one market and one currency is forcing the EU countries to a certain harmonization of their socio-economic policies. This is not to say that it will be an easy conversion; indeed it will be a very complicated procedure, because it involves changing entire economic and social structures. Yet we strongly believe that the sources of conflicts within this particular welfare state regime will in the end result in its dissolution. Not only will the financial costs be too high, the particular division of care responsibilities will be challenged and rejected by a growing number of women.

This leaves two possible alternatives. Of these, the liberal welfare state regime has the great advantage of being more or less 'in tune' with the ideological climate of the 1980s and early 1990s. In general, there is a great distrust of heavy state involvement and a great belief in the sanctity of the market. This corresponds nicely with the basic political premises of the liberal welfare state regime. Also, the central assumption concerning gender relations is difficult to counter. 'Gender' does not seem to play a role in this type of welfare state regime, which may lead to the wrong, but rather convincing conclusion that problems concerning gender relations are solved in a satisfying way. More specifically, this type of welfare state regime seems to be stimulated by the European unification process to a considerable extent. In fact, 'Europe 1992' can be regarded as heavily inspired by 'supply-side-economics', clearing away all assumed excessive regulation in favour of the market.

From women's point of view, however, this particular welfare state regime does not seem very attractive. Indeed the differences among women within this welfare state regime may be rather large. The basic problem, of course, is that care responsibilities remain individualized. The more privileged women will be able to relieve themselves of these responsibilities by hiring services in the market. The less privileged lack the financial resources, and face the difficulty of combining paid and unpaid labour. Class differences therefore will become more central.

This leaves the social democratic welfare state regime. In this regime women are at least treated as individuals, having their own incomes and their own entitlements to social security. In addition, care responsibilities are to a large extent socialized, which gives women the opportunity to combine paid and unpaid labour. There are some doubts, however, whether this particular regime will survive in the long run. The high level of public expenditure may cause problems, especially considering the European unification process (Borchorst 1994). The problem is not that certain provisions are no longer 'in tune' with European regulation, but that the costs of these provisions have to be paid within the straitjacket of European economic and monetary union. In addition, the position of women within this system has been criticized by feminist scholars. The basic concern seems to be that even this particular welfare state regime has not

101

achieved full equality between men and women. There is still a considerable wage gap and the occupational structure is extremely segregated (Lewis and Åström 1992). On the other hand, one might consider that social democratic policy with regard to care has strengthened the autonomy of women and provides a basis for the empowering of women in society (Siim 1991).

So, with some hesitation, the question of whether we are heading towards a convergence can be answered affirmatively. The national particularities will to some extent diminish. Whether this will mean an improvement in the relative position of women is still an open question. Much will depend on the extent to which the involvement of feminist scholars with the welfare state can be converted into actual policy.

REFERENCES

Borchorst, A. (1994) 'The Scandinavian welfare states – patriarchal, gender neutral or woman-friendly?', *International Journal of Contemporary Sociology*, 31(1), pp. 45–68.

Esping-Andersen, G. (1990) *The Three Worlds of Welfare Capitalism*, Cambridge: Polity Press.

Hochschild, A. (with Anne Machung) (1989) *The Second Shift. Working Parents and the Revolution at Home*, New York: Viking.

Juster, F.T. and Stafford, F.P. (1991) 'The allocation of time, empirical findings, behavioral models and problems of measurement', *The Journal of Economic Literature*, 29(2), pp. 471–522.

Langan, M. and Ostner, I. (1991) 'Gender and welfare. Towards a comparative framework', in G.J. Room (ed.) *European Developments in Social Policy*, Bristol: J.W. Arrowsmith.

Lewis, J. (1992) 'Gender and the development of welfare regimes', *Journal of European Social Policy*, 2(3), pp. 159–73.

—— and Åström, G. (1992) 'Equality, difference and state welfare: labour market and family policies in Sweden', *Feminist Studies*, 18(1), pp. 59–87.

O'Connor, J.S. (1993) 'Gender, class and citizenship in the comparative analysis of welfare state regimes: theoretical and methodological issues', *British Journal of Sociology*, 44(3), pp. 501–18.

OECD (1994) 'Shaping structural change. The role of women', in OECD, *Women and Structural Change. New Perspectives*, Paris: OECD.

Orloff, A.S. (1993) 'Gender and the social rights of citizenship: the comparative analysis of gender relations and welfare states', *American Sociological Review*, 58(3), pp. 303–28.

Passchier, C.E. (1992) 'Naar een nieuw "werker profile"', *Sociaal Maandblad Arbeid*, 47(3), pp. 119–25.

Plantenga, J. (1995) 'Labour market participation of women in the European Union', in A. van Doorne-Huiskes, J. van Hoof and E. Roelofs (eds) *Women and the European Labour Markets*, London: Paul Chapman.

Rubery, J. and Fagan, C. (1993) 'Occupational segregation of women and men in the European Community', *Social Europe*, Supplement 3/93, Luxembourg: Office for Official Publications of the European Communities.

Sainsbury, D. (ed.) (1994) *Gendering Welfare States*, London: Sage.

Siim, B. (1991) 'Welfare state, gender politics and equality polities: women's citizenship in the Scandinavian welfare states', in E. Meehan and S. Sevenhuijsen (ed.) *Equality Politics and Gender*, London: Sage.

Statistica Centralbyrån (1992) *I tid och otid. En undersökning om kvinnors och mäns tidsanvändning 1990/1991*, Levnadsforhällanden Rapport 79.

Women in Europe (1992) *The Position of Women on the Labour Market. Trends and Developments in the Twelve Member States of the European Community, 1983–1990*, Supplement no. 36, Brussels: Commission of the European Communities.

7

WOMEN IN THE SOUTH: DIVERSE EXPERIENCES OF WORK IN A UNIFYING EUROPE

Dina Vaiou and Maria Stratigaki

INTRODUCTION

The project of European Integration – and the political, as well as academic, debate around the meanings and extent of 'integration' – has brought to the fore, with renewed intensity, the fact that the benefits of a Single European Market (SEM) will be quite unequally distributed among regions and social groups within the Community. However, earlier policies against such 'malfunctioning' of the European philosophy seem to be gradually being abandoned in practice, as the priorities of the Maastricht Treaty indicate, and the SEM is expected to promote convergence (see, for example, Delors 1988, Kazakos 1989, Malheiros 1990).

However, even the policies which were put in place in the past to counter this 'malfunctioning' had a serious weakness. These policies followed two parallel lines of analysis whose interconnections, which are important for large groups of Europeans and for women in particular, have not been taken on board. On the one hand, analyses and policies dealing with the impact of European integration on regions focused exclusively on economic indicators and the performance of firms, while on the other hand there have been analyses and policies concerning employment, some of which focus on women (mainly through Action Programmes for 'Equal Opportunities for Women and Men') and on the prospects and problems that European integration presents for women. These Programmes touch upon broad and far-reaching aspects of women's lives, but the basic areas of action are limited to promoting a legislative framework for equality and supporting training schemes. These methods of intervention perpetuate a partial focus on women-as-workers in the labour market, while leaving out important aspects of everyday life. Moreover, they are based on assumptions about employment that are not pertinent for many groups of women in Southern Europe.

This chapter seeks to clarify some of the meanings and content that 'work'

104

– mainly, but not exclusively, paid work – has for women in the South. The chapter is based on research in four Southern European countries – Spain, Portugal, Italy and Greece – and on more detailed studies of one region in each country: Anatoliki Makedonia, a region in Northern Greece where the agricultural sector is still quite significant; the Marche, a part of the 'Third Italy' (the Centre-North East) which is close to or slightly above the EU averages for Gross Domestic Product (GDP) per capita and unemployment; Catalunya, a high unemployment industrial region in Spain; and Lisboa e Vale do Tejo, a growing urban region in Portugal (Vaiou et al. 1991).

It is important to emphasize that Southern Europe is, in many ways, very diverse and cannot be approached as one entity. Hence our emphasis on studying *geographically differentiated contexts* of work and everyday life in different types of regions. The premise is that women's prospects, much more than men's, are conditioned by the structure of the particular places to which they are tied. It is also a first attempt to bring together lines of analysis about European integration which are usually kept apart.

The first part of the chapter examines women's participation in the labour force, as it is revealed by statistical and other quantitative surveys. However, this is only a partial account of women's work in Southern Europe. Based on a wide range of 'local' and/or 'sectoral' research, we argue, in the second part of the chapter, that a lot of women's activity lies outside the areas which statistics measure and evaluate. This is one of the reasons why European policies (and national and local policies) have thus far been ineffective. As we argue in the concluding part of the chapter, they will probably continue to be of little relevance for women in the South, unless this unrecorded, unregulated, place-specific volume of work is taken into account.

WOMEN'S PARTICIPATION IN THE LABOUR FORCE: DEVELOPMENTS IN THE 1980S

According to the Labour Force Surveys, women's participation in the labour market increased during the second half of the 1980s in all Southern countries, as in the rest of Europe. This increase resulted from a larger number of women entering both employment and unemployment pools. However, as Table 7.1 indicates, women's activity rates in Spain, Italy and Greece remain much lower than the Eur 12 average, while in Portugal it is much higher, mainly due to the expansion of public services after 1974.

The high percentage of women who remain 'outside' the labour force in Europe, particularly in the South, has recently started to attract the interest of policy makers at an EU level. This is mainly due to the European 'delay' in comparison with its two world competitors, the USA and Japan. The 'non-labour force' represents considerable under-utilized human resources (*Employment in Europe 1992*: Chapter 3), which should be productively utilized.

105

Table 7.1 Women's activity rates, 1993

	Spain	Italy	Greece	Portugal	Eur 12
Activity rate[a]	34	34	35	50	44
Women engaged in non-paid activities[b]	78	74	78	55	63

[a] Women active on the labour market as percentage of women 15 years and more
[b] Includes family workers, unemployed and economically inactive women as percentage of women 15 years and more

Source: Eurostat, Labour Force Survey 1993

Analysis of activity rates by age indicates the age (and, indirectly, the phase in their life-cycle) at which women move in and out of the labour force in each country, as well as some significant differences between the South and the North. In almost all EU countries, activity rates reach their maximum in the age group 20–24, but participation rates vary considerably in the older age groups. In the 'Southern pattern' the percentage of active women declines after the age of marriage and childbirth, with Spain being the most representative example. In the pattern valid in most Northern countries, the activity curve remains high for a much longer part of women's life-cycle (Plantenga in this volume).

The differences in patterns of activity are even more significant if one considers only the women who are paid for their work. In the South (except Portugal), less than 30 per cent of women aged 15 years and more are formally paid for their work, as employees, employers or self-employed. All others are either economically inactive or provide unpaid work within families as family workers[1] (see Table 7.1). Particularly in Greece, family workers account for 25.2 per cent of employed women, while in the European Union on average they account for only 4.3 per cent (figures for 1993). Almost half of these family workers work in the agricultural sector. This sector is constantly declining in the EU, following the restructuring of farm production promoted by the Common Agricultural Policy of the Community. Such a shift implies that a large number of women's employment opportunities – even as family workers – are at risk, especially in geographical areas where very few other opportunities for paid work are being created. This is the case in most rural regions of the South.

Among women employees, the job opportunities and working conditions of those employed in industry are declining in the context of the emerging Single Market. The most vulnerable industries are concentrated in Southern European regions. Most of them are characterized by low labour cost per person and (therefore) high percentages of women's labour. A large proportion of female industrial workers in the four Southern countries work in such industries, in particular in the textile, footwear and clothing industries. Recent developments in the structure of industrial production as a result of European unification have already started to threaten large groups of women wage-earners in industry (Conroy Jackson 1990, Meulders and Plasman 1991).

The numbers of women employees in the service sector, the sector that accounts for the largest part of job creation, are increasing in all EU countries. Quantitative expansion of the sector (and of women's employment), however, has not resulted in a reduction in occupational segregation. Women are concentrated in a small range of new jobs, at the bottom of the occupational hierarchy and job evaluation schemes. Women work in traditional 'female' services, such as education, health services and retail sales, as well as in the modern 'female' services such as banking and tourism. The large-scale implementation of new technologies in the service sector has been facilitated by new ways of organizing work, which have created a large number of new job descriptions, less enriching and more flexible in time and space. These jobs are occupied mainly by women whose opportunities for professional career and job satisfaction are therefore dramatically reduced (Stratigaki 1992, Rubery and Fagan 1993).

In the North, women's increased participation in the economically active population has been associated with the growth of part-time employment (Conroy Jackson 1990). In Southern Europe, part-time work has only recently been regulated and recorded, and therefore covered by labour laws. It has increased mainly in regions where the deregulation of working hours, and the computerization in the service sector, have created higher demand (see for example ORML 1989). Nevertheless, in most Southern regions part-time work is still at quite low levels in comparison to figures in all Northern countries: see Table 7.2. The public sector has, until recently, worked as a partial substitute for part-time work, due to its shorter working hours. The low percentage of part-time work in the South explains, at least in part, the dramatic drop in female activity rates after the age of marriage and childbirth, which contrasts with the pattern in most Northern EU countries. It seems that non-active women in the South 'correspond' to part-timers in the North, at least regarding employment patterns.

Before concluding our discussion of women's participation in the labour force in Southern Europe, two points have to be raised which help to

Table 7.2 Women working part-time as a percentage of all women in employment, 1993

	Spain	Italy	Greece	Portugal	Eur 12
Industry	8.0	8.3	5.2	7.1	19.3
Services	16.4	10.9	6.7	10.8	32.3
Total employment	14.8	11.0	7.6	11.0	29.7

Source: Eurostat, Labour Force Survey 1993

delineate the terms of their activity. First, with the exception of Portugal, unemployment rates among women are (much) higher than the EU average and almost double those of the men in each country (Table 7.3). More than 46 per cent of unemployed women in the EU have been seeking a job for more than twelve months (long-term unemployed), whereas the proportions in Greece, Spain and Italy are considerably higher. In addition, in the context of generally declining job opportunities, women's unemployment rates in the South (except Portugal) have increased more rapidly than their employment rates (Meulders, Plasman, Van der Stricht 1992).

Table 7.3 Unemployment indicators, 1993

Unemployment rate	Spain	Italy	Greece	Portugal	Eur 12
Women	28.6	14.8	13.6	6.3	12.2
Men	18.6	7.7	5.7	4.5	9.5
Long-term unemployed (12 months and more) as a percentage of the unemployed					
Women	55.5	60.3	56.7	40.2	46.5
Men	37.8	55.8	40.7	35.4	41.8

Source: Eurostat, Labour Force Survey 1993

Secondly, economic activity in Southern European countries is diffused over a large number of very small firms in which job security, the conditions of work, unionization, and even the definition and experience of work itself, are very different from those faced by the Northern 'mass worker' in a large factory or office. Examples from the regions that we have studied in detail are illustrative: in the Marche industrial firms average 5 employees per firm. In Catalunya, 70 per cent of industrial firms employ fewer than 10 employees. In Anatoliki Makedonia industrial firms average 15 employees per firm, mainly due to the presence of a few large clothing firms (employing 100–200 people). In commerce, figures fall below 2 employees per firm (1.9 in Marche and Anatoliki Makedonia) – which practically means family shops and/or self-employment. These are important considerations for an analysis of women's work, and for policy formulation.

WORKING WOMEN IN SOUTHERN EUROPE: BEYOND EUROSTAT

Statistical surveys – and reports based exclusively on them – give a partial picture of women's work since they include only part of their money-earning activity, not to mention the heavy load of domestic and unpaid labour. This is particularly true for Southern Europe. The work women do, such as a large part of the agricultural work in family farms, work in small family businesses, industrial work at home, informal and/or seasonal work in tourism, industry or personal services, and irregular work in the public sector, is largely unrecorded, so that they are not classified as 'working persons' or 'economically active'.

A lot of confusion about these other forms of work, and women's involvement in them, arises from two overlapping, but not identical, dichotomies, which are usually present in the debate on work and employment: between formal and informal employment and between typical and atypical employment. It is beyond the scope of this chapter to discuss the vast literature on these issues. The following points of clarification are, however, necessary.

First, 'atypical' employment and 'informal' activities are defined by negation, as 'other' and different from what has been established as 'the norm' in most research and policy making. 'Typical', 'formal' or 'regular', in this context, apply only to lifelong, full-time, male employment for a wage, for large employers in industry and/or the services (Pahl 1988). But this form of employment, although perhaps characteristic of industrial societies, has never become dominant in other parts of the world, including Southern Europe, and even less so among women. Thus an implicit or explicit focus on it creates a hierarchy not only in terms of work but also in terms of workers.

Second, informal activities are very widespread in Southern Europe. Informal activities include traditional forms of production in various sectors, but also activities generated by the restructuring strategies of firms, criminal activities and profitably exploiting the inadequacy of the 'formal' regulatory system (for an elaboration of a typology in Southern Europe see Mingione 1988, Hadjimichalis and Vaiou 1990b). These activities have been approached mainly as a problem of tax evasion, hence the interest of states, central banks, political parties, the OECD, the World Bank and, very recently, the EU. But definitions in terms of recording and taxation overlook the employment relations characteristic of these activities, which can be very unfavourable for workers, with a lack of security and stability, low levels of remuneration, a flexible working regime, and little or no recording and payment of benefits (Pinnaro and Pugliese 1985, Lawson 1992). In addition, such definitions pay little attention to the people involved in these relations, i.e. to social groups who are in a particularly weak position in the labour market on the basis of age (young and old), gender (women) or social origin (ethnic minorities, recent migrants), whose labour is a prerequisite for these informal activities.

Third, 'atypical employment' is a term launched by the EU Network of Experts on 'Women in the Labour Market'. It includes 'all those forms of employment which are distinguished from traditional occupations by characteristics as diverse as the number and distribution of hours worked, the organization and localization of production, wage determination and statutory regulations and conventions' (Meulders and Plasman 1989: 1; see also Chapter 5 of this volume). Following this definition, formal, full-time male employment (re)emerges as the norm (typical) and all other forms of work are defined as 'other' (atypical). Some of these forms of work are registered, at least in part, in EU Labour Force Surveys. Several of them may also be informal, paid or unpaid, at different times and places.

In what follows we discuss some of the more important of those 'other' forms of employment, drawing mainly on our research in the four regions of Southern Europe which we have studied in detail. For some branches of production, atypical forms of employment are part of the traditional way of operating. In most cases, however, they are the result of the restructuring strategies of firms, which have led to the proliferation of small firms, the development of subcontracting networks and a general deregulation of employment, which primarily affects women.

Atypical employment and informal activities in Southern Europe

The exact extent of atypical employment and informal activities is impossible to assess, and the relevant data has to be treated cautiously. This is especially, but by no means exclusively, the case with informal activities which are, by definition, unrecorded (Barthélemy et al. 1988). The importance of atypical forms of employment is therefore usually assessed indirectly from a variety of sectoral or local studies. The bulk of atypical, and largely unrecorded, work is quite heterogeneous, sector-specific in form and place-specific in its concentration. However, some common patterns can be observed, and will be discussed below.

Of all forms of atypical employment in the Meulders and Plasman (1989) classification, only *self-employed* and *family workers* appear in Labour Force Surveys. Extensive use of family workers is very widespread in agriculture, especially where family farming predominates. This, in practice, means women's labour: in the Marche, at the end of the 1980s, 42 per cent of women's labour in agriculture falls in this category, and in Anatoliki Makedonia it exceeds 50 per cent of total labour force in many crops. Family workers are very numerous in the traditional labour-intensive crops, mainly Mediterranean products (vines, olives and citrus) and tobacco (Vaiou et al. 1991: Regional Reports).

Women's work in commerce again takes the form of family labour. The vast majority of businesses are very small (with fewer than two employees) and rely on unpaid family labour for their survival. This is also the case in many tourist businesses, such as restaurants, rooms to let, tourist agencies, entertainment and bathing establishments. In the latter case – where work is also seasonal – women become 'housewives' when the season is over, or engage in agricultural work. It is worth noting that many women registered as housewives (i.e., not in the labour force) actually engage in a multitude of occupations the year round: in farming for part of the year, in tourism during the season, in a family shop for some hours every day, and in housework, without ever gaining the status of a 'working person' (Merelli et al. 1986, Durán 1987, Hadjimichalis and Vaiou 1990a).

A trend that can be observed in both the Marche and the region of Lisboa e Vale do Tejo is the increasing numbers of self-employed women in agriculture (André 1991, Materazzi 1991). This is associated with the transfer of the farm titles to women when men find a job outside agriculture. It has to do more with taxation and bureaucratic transactions than with any real transfer of control to women. Other than this, self-employment is more common among men than among women.

As we have already mentioned, the amount of *part-time* employment, i.e. employment with reduced hours of work, as compared to the legal or conventional ones, is still quite low in most Southern regions. However, reduced or irregular work hours are common in many forms of *temporary employment*, such as 'fixed term', 'casual', 'seasonal', or 'on call' work. Seasonal work is common in agriculture and in agro-industries (mainly tobacco and food processing). If employment is formal (i.e. with a contract), for each country there is a minimum number of working days that entitles workers to unemployment benefits for the rest of the year. Much of the seasonal labour in agriculture, however, is informal, especially during the harvest season. For the labour-intensive crops in Anatoliki Makedonia, women comprise over 80 per cent of the labour force used during the harvest, selection and packing of fruit (Papayannakis et al. 1986, Hadjimichalis and Vaiou 1990a). Most of the seasonal labour in this region (55–65 per cent) is without contracts. In Catalunya the same types of jobs have recently been taken by immigrants from Africa (South-Saharan and Moroccan) (Cruz-Villalón 1987, Garcia-Ramón 1988). In the Vale do Tejo, where the main crops are tomatoes and grapes, women's employment in seasonal jobs is very considerable in harvesting and processing the produce (Ferrão 1985).

Following recent cuts in public expenditure, seasonal or temporary employment has also become common in public services. In Italy and Spain, young women are hired for three months or less once or twice a year in the postal and telephone service, in local government, education, etc., in order to cover special needs without increasing the permanent personnel. In the region of Lisboa, liberalization promoted by government labour policies resulted in a considerable rise in temporary contracts involving mainly women: about 24 per cent of employed women hold such contracts (Vaiou et al. 1991).

Large department stores and tourist facilities also operate on temporary or casual contracts. A number of examples can be mentioned here: in Catalunya, temporary contracts are commonly 'chained' together to cover permanent needs (and corresponding workplaces), with considerable savings for the firms in terms of salaries and fringe benefit contributions (Barthélemy et al. 1988). In the Italian department store 'Standa', seasonal workers, usually the same ones, are hired at peak periods (e.g. Christmas) when the store is open from 8.30 in the morning until 8.00 in the evening. In this store they also employ women on part-time and part-year (6 or 7 months full-time) contracts (ORML 1989).

It is interesting to note that the growth of women's participation in the labour force has contributed to the growth of yet another area of informal work in services, namely *domestic work*. This is almost exclusively performed by women, whether local women or foreign women from Eastern Europe and Third World countries (Vaiou et al. 1991: Regional Reports).

Homeworking is an important part of the operations of a variety of branches in manufacturing, and involves primarily women. According to the Council of Europe (1989), in Southern Europe women constitute 80–90 per cent of the estimated 1.5 million homeworkers. Working at home is a form of atypical employment, with the worst working conditions for women. Women work at home, trying to combine household and childcare tasks with paid work. They are paid on piece rates, which, by itself, makes work very intensive. Working time cannot be separated from time devoted to other tasks. Sometimes the materials used in the manufacture of small articles (toys, Christmas ornaments, shoes, etc.) are dangerous for a child's and adult's health. As a rule, homeworkers do not enjoy social security or other benefits, and employers do not abide by the law which recognizes homeworkers as employees.

In Anatoliki Makedonia and Catalunya, homeworking predominates in the clothing industry, which is an important industry in these regions. It used to be more common in the Marche in the 1970s, but has become less frequent and more regulated since. This is a result of union and government controls and of women's changing attitudes to work (see Benton 1986, Recio et al. 1986, Hadjimichalis and Vaiou 1990a, Vinay 1985). According to research on manufacturing in the Marche, work at home accounts for 3.6 per cent of regional employment in manufacturing, with higher figures in feminized branches (12 per cent in shoes, 13 per cent in musical instruments, 18 per cent in other industries). It must be underlined, however, that these data are based on employers' responses to questionnaires, and should be treated cautiously, like all quantitative data on atypical employment.

Many of the activities described above are *informal* in that they do not involve any contracts and, quite often, do not conform to any labour law in terms of the conditions of work, pay and social security. This type of work is still important in all sectors of economic activity and involves a predominantly female workforce:

- in agriculture, much of the seasonal labour is without contracts;
- the proliferation of family farming, and of small family firms especially in tourism, opens up a significant area of women's unrecorded and sometimes unpaid work;

- subcontracting part of industrial production to homeworkers is a means of coping with international competition for many firms in the clothing, food and toy industries, etc;
- a number of services, such as domestic work, are offered on an informal basis.

Choices and alternatives

Women's concentration in informal and atypical jobs in Southern Europe is by no means a matter of choice. It is, to a large extent, due to the lack of alternatives (full-time, regular jobs) and also due to the lack of the accessible and affordable social infrastructure that would enable them to look for such alternatives. Women's increasing participation in money-earning activities, both registered and informal, has not been matched by the corresponding development of such an infrastructure. Caring and domestic labour remain 'women's work'. It is time- and energy-consuming, discourages entry into the labour market and certainly determines the conditions under which this is possible (see for example, Carfagna 1990, Carretta 1990, David and Vicarelli 1991, Durán 1987, Commission for Equality and Women's Rights 1991, Vaiou and Stratigaki 1989).

Childcare for under-fives still covers only a small proportion of the children in that age group, and the hours covered often do not correspond to working hours. Mothers of young children are then forced out of the labour market, with non-participation rates reaching over 60 per cent. The opening hours of state schools are still based on the assumption that mothers are constantly available to take children to and from school and look after them before or after class, during mid-day breaks and long holidays. Schools are open from 8.00 or 9.00 to 13.00 in Italy and Spain and work in shifts in Greece and Portugal, irrespective of mothers' (or parents') working hours. Other services (e.g. health, shopping, banking) operate on the same assumption, thereby creating the need for a full-time housewife in each household (CREW 1989).

Women have to cope with by far the greatest part of the burden of caring and domestic labour. Their extended 'job' definition includes, for example, making services and facilities available to different members of the household or complementing poor or non-existent public services. They are thus tied to their area of residence and limited in their choices for paid work. The hours of a paid job and the travel time to reach it are an important consideration when the job has to be fitted in with school schedules, looking after an elderly relative or the hours when shops are open and services are available. Some of the pressures are accommodated in old or new forms of the extended family, with older women providing the services that are inadequate or unavailable. Trying to combine paid work and family life creates a whole network of mutual obligations and

113

dependence among women of different ages, while the vast majority of men remain uninvolved.

'SOCIAL PARTNERS': LIMITATIONS OF EUROPEAN POLICY

Both formal and informal women's employment conditions are influenced by recent demographic changes in divorce and fertility rates, and therefore the childcare burden per woman, and by improving levels of educational attainment for women. Recent developments in these fields have improved women's professional opportunities. The total fertility rate in the South has declined considerably over the last thirty years, so that the average household size in Italy, for example, fell below three in the 1980s. At the same time, women's participation in education and vocational training schemes increased in all Southern countries in the 1980s. For example in Spain 62.6 per cent of young women (20–24 years old) have completed secondary schooling, as compared to 62.3 per cent of young men, while 5.5 per cent of the same women have completed tertiary schooling (whether technical or University), as compared to only 3.1 per cent of young men (Vaiou et al. 1991: Regional Reports).

These developments have helped improve the life chances of a minority of women who are well-educated and have access to information and control of their fertility. Some (but by no means all) of these women have been able to obtain high-status jobs and, at the same time, raise a family. They do this by buying services in the market (e.g. help for housework, childcare, caring, etc.) and by relying on family networks for assistance. However, the overall situation for the majority of women has not improved significantly. Living in the less developed regions of the EU, with limited prospects for economic improvement, disadvantages them significantly. In addition, the structure of the labour market has developed in such a way that women's integration has been either in the new low-status jobs in the formal service sector, even when they have high qualifications, or in the new forms of paid work created by the proliferation of informal activities. This would most often be family work in small businesses, or work at home.

Whatever type of job women may be able to obtain, most seem to have only very limited possibilities of improving the conditions of their work. In the formal sector, particularly in unionized branches such as banking, collective bargaining takes place through traditionally organized trade unions in which men dominate the decision-making process. Women, who mainly occupy newly created flexible, part-time jobs, cannot participate in the negotiations which, in the South, aim mainly to safeguard full-time jobs and prevent the expansion of part-time work.

In many economic sectors, even when work is performed formally, unionization is extremely difficult due to the dispersion of employment over a large number of small businesses. Especially in rural areas with declining agricultural production, women who find jobs in small production units do not have the necessary bargaining power. The situation is even more problematic in the case of women working in the informal sector, where not only is unionization not possible but even the implementation and monitoring of labour regulations becomes extremely difficult.

In this context, women in Southern Europe cannot easily be part of the 'social dialogue' at a European or national level, which is an important component of the philosophy and policies for European Integration. Their experience of work is very different from that which underlies the concept of 'social partners', which presumes formal labour relations and collective organizations of workers through which they can be represented in the dialogue with employers. For the many women in the South who are engaged in atypical or informal employment, and who are seldom unionized, social partnership hardly corresponds to the terms and conditions of their work.

All those women are left out of the dialogue: out of the bargaining concerning agricultural policy or the multi-fibre agreement, out of the measures for the improvement of working conditions, social security and workers' protection, out of collective bargaining and other avenues for the promotion of their rights and interests. Those who take part in the social dialogue are, more often than not, men, with completely different experiences of work. Thus women in the South, whose work is not in any way 'typical', are invisible for European policy. However, a significant part of the economic activity in the regions and cities of Southern Europe relies on their labour, and the large volume of unrecorded, invisible labour which they contribute is taken for granted by the 'social partners'. It is taken for granted that they will continue to be the 'unchanging backcloth' of economic and social development and to bear the burden of European Integration under most unfavourable conditions.

NOTE

1   Family workers are persons who help another member of the family to run an agricultural holding or other business, provided they are not considered as employees.

REFERENCES

André, I.M. (1991) 'Women's employment in Portugal', *Iberian Studies*, 20(1/2), pp. 28–41.
Barthélemy, P., Miguelez-Lobo, F., Mingione, E., Pahl, R. and Wenig, A. (1988) *Underground Economy and Irregular Forms of Employment (Travail au Noir)*, Programme for research and action on the development of the labour market (10 vols), DG V, Brussels: Commission of the European Communities.

Benton, L. (1986) 'La informalización del trabajo en la industria', *Papeles de Economía*, 26.

Carfagna, S. (1990) 'La popolazione', ISTAT, *Sintesi Della Vita Sociale Italiana*, Roma, pp. 25–71.

Carretta, M. (1990) 'La famiglia', ISTAT, *Sintesi Della Vita Sociale Italiana*, Roma, pp. 293–344.

Commission for Equality and Women's Rights (1991) *Portugal, Status of Women 1991*, Lisboa.

Conroy Jackson, P. (1990) *The Impact of the Competition of the Internal Market on Women in the European Community*, Working document prepared for DG V, Equal Opportunities Unit (V/506/90–EN), Brussels: Commission of the European Communities.

Council of Europe (1989) *The Protection of Persons Working at Home*, Strasbourg: Council of Europe.

CREW, in collaboration with McLoone, J. and O'Leary, M. (1989) *Infrastructures and Women's Employment*, DG V, Brussels: Commission of the European Communities.

Cruz-Villalón, J. (1987) 'Political and economic change in Spanish agriculture 1950–1985', *Antipode*, 19(2), pp. 119–33.

David, P. and Vicarelli, G. (1991) 'Le donne di Ancona. Una ricerca su modelli sociali, doppia presenza, lavori culture', *Politica ed Economia – Studi e Ricerche*, 7–8, Roma: CESPE.

Delors, J. (1988) *Regional Implications of Economic and Monetary Integration*, Report on the Economic and Monetary Union in the European Community, Collection of papers submitted to the Committee for the study of the EMU, Brussels: Commission of the European Communities.

Durán, M.A. (1987) 'Notas para una crítica de textos básicos de economía española', in *El Trabajo de las Mujeres*, Madrid: Instituto de la Mujer, Ministerio de Cultura.

Employment in Europe 1992 (1992), Luxembourg: Office for Official Publications of the European Communities.

Ferrão, J. (1985) 'Recomposição social e estruturas regionals de classes', *Análise Social*, 21(87–88–89), pp. 565–604.

Garcia-Ramón, M.D. (1988) 'Género y actividad agraria en España: una aproximación a partir del Censo Agrario de 1982', *Documents d'Análisi Geografica*, 13, UAB.

Hadjimichalis, C. and Vaiou, D. (1990a) 'Flexible labour markets and regional development in northern Greece', *International Journal of Urban and Regional Research*, 14(1), pp. 1–24.

—— and —— (1990b) 'Whose flexibility? The politics of informalisation in Southern Europe', *Capital and Class*, 42(4): 79–106.

Kazakos, P. (ed.) (1989) *Greece and the Development of the Internal Market in Europe*, Athens: Ionian Bank (in Greek).

Lawson, V. (1992) 'Industrial subcontracting and employment forms in Latin America: a framework for contextual analysis', *Progress in Human Geography*, 16(1), pp. 1–23.

Malheiros, J.M. (1990) 'Le Portugal, au sud de l'Europe entre la Méditerranée et l'Atlantique', *Sociedade e Território*, No. Special, Lisboa.

Materazzi, R. (1991) 'Donne e mercato del lavoro nelle Marche: alcune riflessioni', *Donne al Lavoro*, Atti della Conferenza Regionale sul lavoro feminile, Regione Marche, Osservatorio Regionale sul Mercato del Lavoro, Ancona: Tecnoprint.

Merelli, M. et al. (1986) *Giochi di Equilibrio. Tra Lavoro e Famiglia le Donne della Cooperazione nel Modello Emiliano*, Milano: Franco Angeli.

Meulders, D. and Plasman, R. (1989) *Women in Atypical Employment*, DG V (V/ 1426/89–FR), Brussels: Commission of the European Communities.

—— and —— (1991) 'The impact of the single market on women's employment in the textile and clothing industry', *Social Europe*, Supplement 2/91, Luxembourg: Office for Official Publications of the European Communities.

——, —— and Van der Stricht, V. (1992) *La Position de Femme sur le Marché du Travail dans la Communauté Européenne* (1983–1990), DG V (V/938/92–FR), Brussels: Commission of the European Communities.

Mingione, E. (1988) 'Work and informal activities in urban Southern Italy', in R. Pahl (ed.) *On Work. Historical, Comparative and Theoretical Approaches*, Oxford: Basil Blackwell.

ORML (Osservatorio Regionale sul Mercato del Lavoro) (1989) *Le Recenti Tendenze del Mercato del Lavoro delle Marche*, Bellettini ORML (no. 10), Ancona: Il Lavoro Editoriale.

Pahl, R. (ed.) (1988) *On Work. Historical, Comparative and Theoretical Approaches*, Oxford: Basil Blackwell.

Papayannakis, L., Hadjantonis, D., Hadjimichalis, C. and Manolopoulos, N. (1986) *Investment Opportunities in Anatoliki Macedonia and Thraki*, Athens: METEK (in Greek).

Pinnaro, G. and Pugliese, E. (1985) 'Informalisation and social resistance: the case of Naples', in N. Redclift and E. Mingione (eds) *Beyond Employment*, Oxford: Basil Blackwell.

Recio, A., Miguelez, F. and Alos, R. (1988) *El Trabajo Precario en Catalunya: la Industria Textil Lanera des Valles Occidental*, Barcelona: Commission Obrera Nacional de Catalunya.

Rubery, J. and Fagan, C. (1993) 'Occupational segregation of women and men in the European Community', *Social Europe*, Supplement 3/93, Luxembourg: Office for Official Publications of the European Communities.

Stratigaki, M. (1992) *Computerisation and Gender Division of Labour in Greek Banking: The Case of the National Bank of Greece*. Ph.D. dissertation, Thessaloniki University, Greece.

Vaiou, D., Georgiou, Z. and Stratigaki, M. (1991) *Women of the South in European Integration: Problems and Prospects*, DG V (V/694/92–EN), in collaboration with P. Vinay, G. Melchiorre (Italy), M. Solsona, L. Suarez, R. Treviño (Spain), I.M. André, C. Ferreira, M.E. Arroz (Portugal), Brussels: Commission of the European Communities.

Vaiou, D. and Stratigaki, M. (guest eds) (1989) 'Women's work: between two worlds', Special issue *Synchroma Themata*, No. 40 (in Greek).

Vinay, P. (1985) 'Family life cycle and the informal economy in Central Italy', *International Journal of Urban and Regional Research*, 9(1), pp. 82–98.

8

WOMEN IN CENTRAL AND EASTERN EUROPE: A LABOUR MARKET IN TRANSITION

A. Geske Dijkstra

INTRODUCTION

In 1989 the communist system in Central and Eastern European countries broke down. As a result their political and economic systems, ideologies and international relations have been reshaped. Their economies are in the process of moving from centrally planned systems to market economies. This is an all-embracing and sometimes painful transformation. It involves liberalization of the former bureaucratic management of the economy, stabilization of demand, privatization of former state-owned enterprises and economic restructuring.

This chapter assesses what happened and will happen to the situation of women in the labour market during this transformation process. The situation of women in communist Europe appeared very different from that in the West. Female participation in the labour market was high. This was mainly due to two factors:

- the communist ideology, which promoted 'equality' of the sexes;
- labour market policies which promoted 'full employment', including full female employment.

The communist ideology has now lost its influence, and gender equality can be expected to have lost its importance as an official objective. In a market economy, and during the transition to a market economy, full employment is no longer guaranteed. The economic restructuring process that is under way also changes the relative positions of men and women in the labour market in many respects.

Some authors argue that Eastern European women, in the period prior to 1989, had reached equality in the workplace, but that they found themselves overburdened with household work. In the West, they maintain, women faced the opposite problem: greater availability of household appliances and men's increasing help with household tasks relieved women from traditional home-making tasks, but women were still overrepresented in subordinate positions in the labour market (Giele 1992: 9). This dichotomy is far too simple, however. Women in the West had not achieved an equal division of household tasks, nor had women in Central and Eastern Europe reached equality in the labour market. In both capitalist countries and the former socialist countries, there appears to be a strong interaction between the position of women in the labour market and the sexual division of tasks in the household. In Western countries, the fact that women still have the primary responsibility for the household and for raising children limits their careers and explains why women are still underrepresented in the labour market and, in particular, in higher-status jobs (Hochschild 1989). For former communist Europe, it will be shown that the high domestic burden of women can explain their relatively poor position in the labour market before 1990, in spite of their high participation rate. Moreover, this interaction provides clues for assessing the position of women in the labour market during and after the transition.

In the first part of this chapter, the labour market situation of women before the changes of 1989 will be described and analysed. The following section is devoted to the transformation process and its impact on the labour market. Then we turn to an analysis of the impact of this transformation on the situation of women in the labour market. Because figures after 1989 are scarce these projections draw heavily on the argument in the former sections. The chapter ends with a short summary of the most important findings.

WOMEN IN CENTRAL AND EASTERN EUROPE BEFORE THE TRANSFORMATION

The labour market under socialism was very different from that under capitalism: demand for labour was much higher, and effective labour supply was lower. The higher labour demand was caused by economic strategy and by the economic system.[1] All centrally planned countries followed a labour-intensive industrialization strategy: production increases had to come from setting to work as much labour as possible. Wages were low, which did not stimulate labour-saving investment and kept demand for labour high.

The economic system supposed that firms did not have to worry about demand for their products, but rather had to fulfil production plans. To that end, they competed with other firms for resources (production inputs) including labour. Since all firms tried to get hold of as many resources as possible, resources were scarce. At the same time, not all resources could be used productively within the firm: some were idle because of a lack of complementary inputs. As a result there was labour hoarding on a large scale, while the number of vacancies was also high. The labour-intensive strategy, coupled with the high incidence of hoarding, caused low labour productivity.

119

Labour supply in communist Europe was, in principle, not lower than in the West, but *effective* labour supply was lower (Gora 1991). This was due to the attractiveness of the 'parallel economy'. The parallel economy is defined here to include not only informal earning activities, but also the queuing for goods. The attractiveness of parallel activities was caused by the chronic shortages of consumer goods.[2] Workers were motivated to maintain their official job for the security of a basic income and other secondary provisions, such as free health care. But they also worked after, and often during, official working hours in a parallel job, as a typist, taxi driver, or doing furniture repairs, for example. They also spent many 'working' hours queuing. Not surprisingly, the low effective labour supply further reduced labour productivity.

The result of both supply and demand factors was that, officially, there was full employment. In practice, there was a large amount of *hidden unemployment* and high absenteeism. Wages and labour productivity were low.

Female labour market participation

The labour-intensive strategy followed by centrally planned economies made it important to hire as many workers as possible, including female workers. From about 1950, governments stressed equality between men and women, and encouraged women to follow the same education as men and to fulfil equal roles in the labour market. In practice, the strongest motivation for women to participate in the labour market was the generally low wages for everyone, which required two income-earners to make a reasonable family income.

As a consequence, female labour market participation increased, to reach figures of 40 per cent and more of the total workforce by 1970 in Bulgaria, Czechoslovakia, the German Democratic Republic (GDR), Hungary and Poland (see Table 8.1). Although the labour market participation of women

Table 8.1 Women as a proportion of the socialized sector of the labour force, 1950–88

	Bulgaria	Czechoslovakia	GDR	Hungary	Poland	OECD
1950	27.4[a]	38.4	38.4	–	33.0[b]	31.4
1960	33.5	42.8	44.3	32.5	32.8	33.6
1970	41.0	46.7	47.7	40.6	40.0	35.2[c]
1980	47.1	45.4	51.0	45.7[d]	44.5	38.7
1988	49.5[e]	46.0	50.3	46.0[e]	46.8	41.6[f]

[a] 1951, [b] 1955, [c] 1971, [d] 1985, [e] 1986, [f] 1989

Source: Wolchik (1992). For OECD: Paukert (1991)

also increased in OECD countries, it was a more gradual process. Their share of the total workforce did not reach 40 per cent until the 1980s. By 1985, female labour market participation in centrally planned economies was still higher than in most OECD countries. The average ratio of women's to men's labour force participation was 80 per cent for Eastern Europe, while it was 64 per cent for the advanced industrialized nations (Blau and Ferber 1992: 30). Figure 8.1 shows the female participation curve (labour market participation according to age) for Poland. It is clear that the form of the curve indicates the Scandinavian participation pattern: a high and uninterrupted bell or inverted U-curve (see Plantenga in this volume). It can be assumed that this was the regular pattern in the former centrally planned economies.

It is important to note that the factors that stimulated female labour market participation in OECD countries were somewhat different from those in Central and Eastern Europe (Paukert 1991, Wolchik 1992). In the West, after the Second World War, national income increased rapidly which led to an expanding service sector in which many women were employed. The increased income also led to more production and consumption of household appliances, which reduced the amount of time necessary for household activities. The increased labour market participation of women was a gradual process, and it was accompanied by gradually decreasing birth rates. Finally, these factors were supplemented by ideological changes, in particular, the notion that women should not only work within the

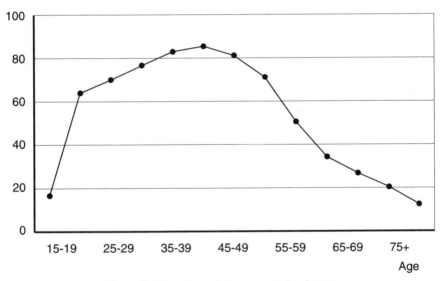

Figure 8.1 Female activity rates, Poland 1991

Source: ILO (1991)

household but also should fulfil other roles in society. In the 1970s, 'equality' became an important objective for the women's movement, meaning not only an equal position in the labour market but also an equal sharing of household chores. Although not much has changed since then, in practice, with respect to the division of household tasks, there is at least the beginning of an ideological change.

In the East, female participation in the labour market came about more abruptly. It was not accompanied by lighter household burdens. Although most governments provided school meals and expanded childcare and pre-school facilities, childcare coverage, in particular, was still limited.[3] Household appliances such as washing machines were not available. Since women still had to do the lion's share of household and caring activities, they reacted by having fewer children. As governments became worried about the low birth rates, they took measures to reduce the domestic work load. Some, as in Poland and Czechoslovakia, provided more state assistance for mothers, such as paid maternity leave, a right to withdraw from the labour market for some years while receiving a low wage but maintaining a claim to their former jobs. Others, as in Romania, restricted abortion (Jankubowska 1992: 8, Wolchik 1992: 126). Birth rates do not seem to have increased much, however.

Although state policies in the former communist countries were important in stimulating female labour market supply, they also weakened the position of women relative to that in the West. The planners' low priority for consumer goods prevented household appliances becoming available, and the 'equality' concept focused only on access to paid work, and did not imply any consequences for the division of caring and household tasks. Given the authoritarian political system, this meant that the existing gender ideology that women were responsible for household chores and child-rearing was reinforced.[4]

What figures we do have on the division of household chores in the former communist countries show that it was unequal indeed. Men in Poland did not do any work at home (ILO 1992). 1986 figures for Hungary show that women did the majority of various types of domestic activity, such as shopping, cooking, washing dishes, cleaning, laundry and ironing, even if they were active breadwinners (and most women were). Only in carrying out repairs were men the most active (Women of Hungary 1991). This is in line with the traditional vision of gender roles in the household.

Labour market conditions of women

Apart from the participation rate, the characteristics of female labour and the relative wages of women are important. Where were women employed? Was the demand for female labour concentrated in a few sectors, or was it generalized? What was the ratio between male and female earnings?

122

Figures for Central and Eastern Europe indicate that horizontal segregation was high, although on average a bit lower than in advanced industrial countries. The average segregation index, indicating the percentage of men or women who would have to change jobs to make the distribution of men and women by occupational category the same, was 31.3 per cent in Eastern Europe, versus 39.5 per cent in industrialized countries (Table 8.2). Table 8.3 shows that, as in the West, women were overrepresented in services. Commercial services such as trade, restaurants, transport, communications, and finance and insurance were relatively underdeveloped in Central and Eastern Europe, but publicly provided services were important. More women worked in manufacturing than in OECD countries. Within manufacturing, female workers dominated the so-called light (consumer goods) industries.

Figures for former Czechoslovakia show that clothing, leather and footwear, tobacco and ceramics were the sectors with the highest share of female workers (Paukert 1991). These sectors had a low relative priority in industrial strategy: investment was low and machinery was obsolete, and, not surprisingly, wages were low. Female workers were relatively underrepresented in heavy industry. They did make up, however, a large part of the white collar workers in that sector (Paukert 1991). This can be explained by the fact that firms' directors aimed at achieving the largest possible wage fund by attempting to hire as many workers as possible. This means they had an incentive to hire low-paid female workers for administrative jobs. Since heavy industry took priority in the socialist strategy, this sector was important in terms of employment opportunities for women. In Czechoslovakia, for example, although females accounted for only 24.2 per cent of employment in the non-electrical machinery field, this industry represented 19.2 per cent of total manufacturing employment. As a consequence, this branch employed in absolute numbers more women than all other manufacturing branches.[5]

The high labour market participation of women did not lead to a change in the organization of paid work. Almost all women worked full-time. In Hungary, for example, only 3 per cent of women worked part-time, and 6 per cent in some kind of freelance work (Women of Hungary 1991: 17). State policies to provide childcare, and, perhaps even more important, to allow for parental leave, seem to have led to this result. In Czechoslovakia, working hours in light industry, where most women worked, were even longer than in heavy industry (44.7 and 41.7 in 1988, respectively). But 70 per cent of the women reported that it was not too difficult to leave the workplace to do some shopping (Paukert 1991: 624).

Table 8.4 shows the earnings differential between men and women by broad occupational category for several Central and Eastern European countries in 1980. It proved to be of about the same magnitude as in advanced industrialized countries. For a number of reasons, this is an

Table 8.2 Occupational segregation by major occupational category for Central and Eastern European countries, and for the advanced industrialized countries, 1980s[a]

Country	Occupational segregation index
Central and Eastern Europe	**31.3**
Bulgaria	26.2
Czechoslovakia	32.7[b]
Hungary	34.8
Poland	30.7[b]
Yugoslavia	32.1
Advanced Industrialized Nations	**39.5**
Australia	31.9
Austria	44.5
Belgium	38.5
Canada	39.8
Denmark	48.0
Finland	42.7
France	38.4
Germany, Federal Republic	36.9
Gibraltar	42.4
Greece	25.4
Ireland	49.3
Israel	42.1
Japan	23.2
Luxembourg	48.9
Netherlands	38.5
New Zealand	41.5
Norway	46.3
Portugal	26.0
South Africa	45.6
Spain	36.4
Sweden	41.7
Switzerland	39.3
United Kingdom	44.5
United States	36.6

[a] Data is for the 1980s, unless otherwise indicated
[b] Data is for the 1970s

Source: Blau and Ferber (1992)

unexpected result. First, as stated above, there was a bit less horizontal segregation in Central and Eastern European countries. Second, the aim of increasing female education was fairly successful. More often than in the West, women followed vocationally oriented education. This was enhanced by state allocation of young people to educational streams.[6] The numbers of female engineers, doctors and economists were much higher than in the West (Posadskaya 1992, Rudolph et al. 1990). The majority of physicians

Table 8.3 Employment by industry and by sex in Central and Eastern Europe in 1989, in per cent[a]

	Bulgaria[b]		Czechoslovakia[c]		Hungary		Poland		Romania		OECD	
	Total	Share of women[d]	Total	Share of women	Total	Share of women[b]	Total	Share of women[e]	Total	Share of women	Total	Share of women
Agriculture	19	47	12	38	20	39	27	48	28	56	8	40
Industry	38	49	38	41	30	43	29	37	38	42	23	31
Construction	8	21	10	18	7	19	8	20	7	14	7	9
Services	34	59	41	61	43	56	36	61	27	46	63	49
Trade, restaurants and hotels	9	65	11	73	11	65	9	70	6	63	20	47
Transport, storage and communications	7	28	7	33	8	29	6	31	7	17	6	22
Finance, insurance, real estate, etc.	1	82	1	78	1	–	1	85	0	61	9	49
Community, social and personal services[f]	18	68	21	64	22	61[g]	18	66	13	56	27	57
Other	1	57	2	51	1	–	2	44	1	43	0	36
Total	100	50	100	47	100	46	100	46	100	45	100	42

[a] For the Central and Eastern European countries, excluding women on maternity leave
[b] 1988
[c] Includes secondary jobs
[d] State sector only
[e] State sector only, except for agriculture and for total
[f] Except for the OECD total, includes employment in real estate services
[g] Includes employment in 'Finance, insurance, real estate, etc.'

Source: OECD (1991)

and teachers were women. However, this seems to have reduced the wages and status of these jobs: relative wages for these professions were lower than in the West.

The large earnings gap between men and women in Central and Eastern Europe can to a large extent be explained by the persistence of norms and values regarding gender roles, according to which the primary task for women is raising children. There is not much difference between Eastern and Western Europe in this respect. The fact that the parental leave facility was almost entirely used by women, so that many women actually withdrew from the labour market for some years (although not visible in the statistics), also weakened their career possibilities. In spite of their relatively high general education level, very few women held management positions. Officially, women held 30 per cent of the managerial positions, but this implied lower-level management in most of the cases (Heinen 1994: 312).

As in industrialized countries, the reasons for the limited upward mobility of women as compared to men include both a practical and a cultural problem. Managers have to be available for more than the standard number of hours. Since women have the primary responsibility for the household and childcare, this may be a sufficient reason for them not to pursue a leadership position. The cultural factor is that neither men nor women are inclined to accept women in management positions, nor do the candidate female managers see it as a normal career path. Since the traditional concept of gender roles was even more dominant among the populations of Central and Eastern European countries, this factor may have been stronger than in the West. In the former communist countries, an additional reason is that vertical mobility depended not only on one's capacity for the job, but also on loyalty to the Communist Party. Perceived loyalty was probably even more important than capability, and one important indicator of loyalty was availability for party work outside normal working hours.

In conclusion, it is true that labour market participation in Central and Eastern Europe was higher than in advanced industrialized nations. However, the degree of horizontal and, in particular, vertical segregation in the labour market was high: women in higher positions were very scarce and most women worked in lower-paid jobs. The state promoted

Table 8.4 Earnings differentials by occupation and sex (male earnings = 100), 1980

	Bulgaria	Czechoslovakia	Poland	Hungary	GDR
Professionals	78	73	79	77	83
Administrative and clerical workers	75	65	76	74	68
Skilled workers	81	66	70	78	84
Unskilled workers	83	61	74	77	81

Source: ILO 1987 (elaboration of Table 8.2)

women's participation in the labour market by setting low wages generally, by allowing parental leave, and by providing facilities to shoulder part of the household and caring burden of women. These policies, however, were only directed at increasing the number of women in paid work. As a result, there was no change in the organization of work, and hardly any change in opinions and values on the primary task of women. This, in turn, can largely explain the persistent inequality of the labour market position of women.

THE TRANSFORMATION AND ITS IMPACT IN THE LABOUR MARKET

In general, we can expect the transformation to lead to increased unemployment as the result of two opposing trends: a fall in demand for labour and an increase in supply.

Labour supply in the formal sector can be expected to increase (Gora 1991). This is a movement along the supply curve induced by the decline in real wages caused by the transformation. In principle, this wage reduction may lead to an income effect and a substitution effect. As a result of the income effect, labour supply increases. The substitution effect might stimulate workers to supply labour to the parallel economy. In practice, this substitution effect has been low. The transformation to a market economy has so far brought about a decrease in the attractiveness of the parallel economy. As a result of price liberalization, prices have increased and there is no need or demand for parallel activities. In addition, the price increases have reduced demand for goods and services and so put an end to shortages; as a result, there is no need to queue during official working hours.

The demand for labour is falling as a result of shifts in the demand curve itself. A first factor is the recession which overcame the countries in transition after 1989. Production declined in all Central and Eastern European countries. Internally, the transformation to a market economy involved strict demand management policies, such as restricting wages and government expenditure. Externally, demand for their products declined because the CMEA (Council for Mutual Economic Assistance or Comecon) collapsed as a result of the requirement that trade should be paid for in dollars. Other factors were the unification of Germany which reduced demand from the former GDR to zero, and, for some countries, the Gulf war which also limited exports from the former communist countries (OECD 1992: 125). Demand from OECD countries increased somewhat, but could not compensate completely for the export fall.

The second factor reducing labour demand is the change in economic systems. It can be expected that, as a result of increased competition and a hardening of the soft budget constraint, firms are forced to reduce hidden

Table 8.5 GDP growth and unemployment rates, several years

	GDP growth, in %, at constant prices					Unemployment in %				
	90	91	92	93	mid-94	90	91	92	93	mid-94
Poland	−11.6	−7.6	2.6	3.8	4.5	6	12	14	16	17
Czechoslovakia	−0.4	−15.9	−8.5	−	−	−	−	−	−	−
Czechia	−	−	−	−0.3	1.5	1	4	3	4	4
Slovakia	−	−	−	−4.1	−	2	12	10	14	14
Hungary	−3.5	−9.9	−5.1	−2.0	1.0	2	8	12	12	11
Bulgaria	−9.1	−11.7	−5.7	−4.2	−2.0	1	11	15	16	13
Romania	−7.4	−15.1	−13.5	−	−	1	3	6	9	11
Russia	−	−13.0	−19.0	−12.0	−12.0	−	−	5	5	6

Source: IMF 1994

unemployment and to increase average labour productivity by firing superfluous workers. However, these changes have come with some time lag. In some countries, enterprises still seem to enjoy a soft budget constraint. Firms begin the adjustment by reducing working hours, and it takes a while before bankruptcies and dismissals occur on a large scale. The slow change in this respect has cushioned the effect of the recession to some extent. Unemployment figures in some countries are still moderate in comparison with the magnitude of the fall in production (Table 8.5). In the countries that started earlier and are further ahead with the transformation (Poland and Hungary, for example) unemployment rates are higher than in Romania and Russia. However, in the latter countries unemployment can be expected to increase soon.

In countries that are further ahead with the transformation, demand for labour from the private sector, especially from small private firms, will increase. This increase in employment is not always reflected in the official unemployment figures, for example in Poland (Berg 1994). Positive effects on production are, obviously, the intention of the system change. A large restructuring of the economy is meant to come about: large enterprises will be split up into smaller ones, firms will be closed, branches will (almost) disappear and others will come into existence, occupations will disappear and new occupations will emerge. All this requires great mobility and flexibility from workers. Some institutional characteristics of the former centrally planned economies tend to limit this flexibility and mobility: housing shortages, the fact that social security and provisions such as health care were linked to one's job, and the fact that workers have been used to job security for so many years.[7]

For the short term, it can be concluded that unemployment will remain high. It is difficult to predict other labour conditions. But, since unemployment rates will remain high for some time to come, wages will also remain low. Even if the emerging private sector recruits labour on a large scale, wages will remain low because of the high competition these enterprises experience, and the fact that labour unions will probably not yet be active in these small firms. It can be expected that unemployment benefits will be low, too. In Poland, these benefits were relatively generous in 1990, but they gradually declined thereafter (Brown 1992). The main reason is that with rising unemployment levels, neither governments nor firms have sufficient means to support generous schemes.

CONSEQUENCES FOR WOMEN

Now we turn to the question of how women are affected by the transformation and restructuring process. At this point, it is difficult to answer this question. There is not much data available, and what data is available is not very reliable. We must base our analysis partly on data and partly on arguments and assessments derived from the analysis so far.

By 1993, female unemployment rates were higher than male rates in most Central and Eastern European countries; an exception is Hungary (Figure 8.2). Unemployment rates for women range between 5 and 17 per cent. In none of these countries, however, was female unemployment as high as in Spain. Given the expected persistence of high overall unemployment rates in the transitional economies, female unemployment rates are likely to remain high or increase, too.

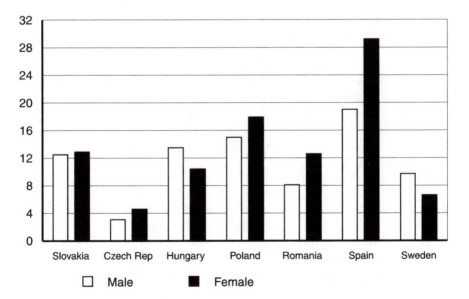

Figure 8.2 Male and female employment rates, 1993

Source: ILO (1995)

129

Female labour *supply* is influenced by many factors, such as the wage level, the unemployment level (a high unemployment level will lower the chance of finding a job and thus discourage job seeking), men's contribution to household tasks, the number of children women have, state policies to relieve the household and childcare burden, the availability of household appliances, and social norms and values on female labour market participation. Some of these factors are not affected by the transformation, at least not in the short or medium term. The number of children is given. We assume that men's contribution to household chores will remain limited, that household appliances will not become available on a large scale soon, and that traditional views on the gender division of unpaid work will continue to prevail.

Some other factors are, however, subject to change. State propaganda to promote 'equality', meaning that women should participate in the labour market, ended. Since the official gender ideology was perceived to be part of the repressive system, and in Eastern Europe also as part of foreign (Soviet) domination, opposition to communist governments was almost automatically linked with ideas such as the right of women to stay at home. So for some, the traditional gender ideology has even been reinforced by the system change (Jankubowska 1992: 10; Rudolph et al. 1990: 38). In many former communist countries, state provisions to facilitate female labour market participation were also affected by the transformation. Governments reduced their expenditures on public childcare, and the cost of these facilities increased (Wolchik 1992: 134; Heinen 1994: 317). In some countries, for example in the former GDR, childcare used to be provided by enterprises; since the enterprises have run out of cash, many kindergartens have closed. The high unemployment rate can be expected to reduce female labour supply even more, because of its discouragement effect.

All factors mentioned so far, both the continuing and the changing ones, work in the same direction: they make women likely to reduce their participation in the labour market. However, wage rates that remain low or will become even lower will probably be important in keeping women in the labour market.

From various surveys in almost all former communist countries in Central and Eastern Europe, carried out before the 1989 changes, we know that the large majority of women worked primarily for economic reasons. But many women also indicated they would continue working even if their husbands made enough money to maintain the family (see Wolchik 1992: 134). In the former Czechoslovakia, a 1991 International Labour Organization (ILO) survey revealed that 76 per cent of the women worked for economic reasons (Paukert 1991: 620–1). Only 7 per cent of the women were said to work for reasons such as interest in the job, the satisfaction of using their abilities or the social environment. The survey also revealed that 28 per cent of the married or cohabiting women would give up their job if the partner's salary increased sufficiently. Apparently, many women (i.e. the other 72 per cent) are now accustomed to employment, and they do not want to change their lives in this respect.[8] Since real wage levels will remain low for some time to come and unemployment benefits will be low too, we can expect that economic reasons will remain important. Even in countries where the general income level is now rising, a large number of women will probably continue working.

In conclusion, both because of the low wage rate and because of the apparent preferences of most women, it is unlikely that female labour supply will decline much during the transformation period. Some discouragement because of the high unemployment rate cannot be excluded, however.

The *demand* for female labour can be analysed at two levels: at a sectoral level, by looking at the prospects for the sectors in which women are currently overrepresented and the possibilities for women to work in new sectors; and at the individual level, by analysing the relative likelihood that women, as compared to men, will remain employed or be hired by employers in the period of transition to a market economy.

With respect to manufacturing, we saw that the prospects for heavy industry are not very good. These firms used to produce for the domestic market or the regional (Eastern European) market. Production in this sector is capital-intensive by nature, and it will be difficult to compete with advanced industrialized nations. It can be expected that the first workers to be dismissed from these enterprises will be women, who make up most of the administrative workers. The incentive to hire as many low-paid female workers as possible does not exist any more.

Women were also overrepresented in the production of manufactured consumer goods. For this 'light industry' the prospects are better. This sector needs investment to replace obsolete machinery, but production is more labour-intensive and the former communist countries of Central and Eastern Europe can, in principle, be competitive because of its lower wage level. Provided investment takes place, there are possibilities for women to retain their jobs in this sector. The lower relative female unemployment rate in Hungary can probably be explained by the fact that these female-dominated sectors did relatively well in that country (Heinen 1994).

Another area with potential opportunities for women is the service sector. Commercial services, which were underdeveloped in the former communist countries, will grow rapidly. Expansion can be expected, for example, in trade, tourism, banking and insurance services, marketing and management consultancy bureaus, legal services for firms and industrial design. Since women make up a large part of the current workforce in services, they can benefit from this expansion. On the other hand, employment in *public* services will probably decrease because of the budgetary restrictions for governments. This will affect female employment opportunities negatively.

On the individual level, a positive factor for women is their relatively high and more job-oriented education level. At the same time, many employers will consider female workers as more expensive and less reliable. Women *are* more expensive because they enjoy secondary benefits such as generous maternity leave. Paradoxically, a reduction in these secondary benefits could have positive effects on women's employment possibilities. Their reputation for unreliability arises from women's higher absenteeism than men in the past, for reasons such as buying food and other necessities for the household, or caring for a sick child. As explained before, this was due to the fact that women have the main responsibility for the household. Current practice shows that advertisements for vacancies are often gender-specific (Einhorn 1993: 8). In Hungary, two-thirds of the vacancies registered at labour offices proved to be 'only for men'. In addition, it is quite normal in that country for advertisements to include a picture of a man (Women of Hungary 1991: 41). Again because they have the primary responsibility for the household, women, more than men, lack mobility and flexibility – two characteristics necessary to take advantage of restructuring processes. They may be unable to move or to register for retraining schemes because of commitments to their family or their partner's job.

The fact that women still have the main responsibility for the household and for raising children will also make it more difficult for women to set up new private businesses. Women, especially women with young children, are unlikely to be able to work the long days required to survive as a private enterprise. According to the 1991 ILO survey in Czechoslovakia, 14 per cent of men and only 7 per cent of women had started or were about to start a small business activity (Paukert 1991: 629). This will also prevent women taking advantage of opportunities in the newly emerging commercial sector: these enterprises must still be created and women are not likely to be the first to do so.

In summary, although many women will lose their jobs, particularly women employed in public services and in heavy industry, there are also some opportunities for women in the labour market, especially in the new sector of commercial services and in consumer goods manufacturing. However, experiences with restructuring processes elsewhere show that, in periods of high unemployment, women tend to be driven out of the better-paid jobs, particularly in manufacturing. Sometimes employers discriminate consciously against women, sometimes women are not considered for retraining schemes, and sometimes they are not able to benefit from new opportunities because of their primary commitment to the family and consequent lack of mobility. In Central and Eastern Europe, the situation seems even worse. More than in the West, views prevail that women are responsible for the household and that they are more expensive and less reliable workers. These factors make prospects for women even bleaker than in other countries or regions.

Prospects for the male–female wage differentials are not very bright either. Experience in the West shows that there is more wage inequality in the private sector than in the public sector. In addition, a link seems to have been confirmed between the overall wage inequality and gender inequality (Blau and Ferber 1992: 37). Since the private sector is likely to expand in the transitional economies of Central and Eastern Europe, leading to higher wage differentials, the earnings gap between men and women will probably also increase. To the extent that women in these countries benefited from the standard wage scales used in the public sector and in state enterprises, they will lose that advantage. Moreover, given the high overall unemployment rate, it can be expected that the share of low-paid, occasional and seasonal work will increase, and that women, as everywhere, are most likely to carry out these kinds of unstable and precarious employment.

At the same time, there are some opportunities in commercial services to earn a relatively high wage. Moreover, education and experience will probably become more important in determining career possibilities and earnings, where previously political loyalty, tradition and seniority counted. This will probably favour women relatively more than men. Highly educated women particularly will be able to benefit from these opportunities. As a result, the income inequality between women will increase.

CONCLUSION

A picture emerges of greater overall inequality of income and employment possibilities, a greater inequality between women, and a greater inequality between men and women. Some workers, including some women, will be able to take advantage of the new opportunities, many others will experience insecurity of employment and income. It can be expected that relatively more women than men will be in the latter position.

The basis for this conclusion is that the official policies of the socialist governments of Central and Eastern Europe to promote 'equality' between the sexes were only directed to increasing the participation of women in paid work. They were enforced from above, and left traditional norms and values regarding the primary responsibility of women in the household largely intact. No change came about in the division of work within the family, and state policies only succeeded in increasing female labour market participation in an unchanged employment framework. They did not lead to an equal position in the labour market for women: both horizontal and vertical segregation in the labour market remained strong.

More than forty years of official promotion of gender equality have led to better education for women, to childcare facilities and to guaranteed jobs; but this policy left women with unchanged husbands and employers, and with a heavy double burden. So the starting point for women at the beginning of a complex restructuring process of the economy is not very good. The only 'asset' which at least some women have is their good education. This will not be enough to face the new situation, in which guaranteed jobs no longer exist and childcare facilities are minimized.

NOTES

1 The economic system is defined here as the institutional structure that determines who takes decisions on production, consumption and distribution. The two extremes are the market economy, with co-ordination by the market and private ownership of the means of production, and centrally planned economies, with co-ordination of decisions by administrative planning and state ownership of the means of production. See Dijkstra (1992).
2 This was, in turn, caused by fixed prices and the fact that firms' demand was not restricted (the 'soft budget constraint' of the firms). See Kornai (1980).
3 The capacity of childcare facilities (day nurseries for children 0–3 years of age) was never more than 11–15 per cent in Bulgaria and Hungary, for example, and was only about 5 per cent in Poland. The capacity of pre-school facilities (for children aged 3–6 years) was higher, namely 70–90 per cent of all children in that age group by the end of the 1980s, except for Poland where it was lower (Heinen 1994: 22).
4 In fact, as Rudolph et al. (1990: 37) showed for Eastern Germany, the collective cleaning and meal services, and state childcare were always carried out by women.
5 Calculated on the basis of figures from Paukert (1991).
6 For example in Czechoslovakia, see Paukert (1991) and in East Germany, see Rudolph et al. (1990). However, Wolchik (1992) states that women more often than men chose only *general* secondary education, and not job-oriented education, so the education of men and women does not seem to have been completely equal.
7 Brown (1992) describes some additional factors for Poland: high wage taxes and the centralized wage bargaining system, which prevents wage levels being determined by productivity.
8 This question was also asked to the partners. Forty-six per cent of them said that they would like their companion to stay at home if their income was high enough (Paukert 1991: 621). What influence these partners will have on female labour supply is unclear, however.

REFERENCES

Berg, A. (1994) 'Does macroeconomic reform cause structural adjustment? Lessons from Poland', *Journal of Comparative Economics*, 18(3), pp. 376–409.
Blau, F.D. and Ferber, M.A. (1992) 'Women's work, women's lives: a comparative economic perspective', in H. Kahne and J.Z. Giele (eds) *Women's Work and Women's Lives: The Continuing Struggle Worldwide*, Boulder, Co.: Westview Press.
Brown, B. (1992) 'Transforming postcommunist labor markets: the Polish case', *RFE/RL Research Report*, 1(32), pp. 50–6.
Dijkstra, G. (1992) *Industrialization in Sandinista Nicaragua: Policy and Practice in a Mixed Economy*, Boulder, Co.: Westview Press.

Einhorn, B. (1993) 'Gender issues in transition: the East Central European experience', Paper to the VIIth General Conference of EADI, Berlin, 15–18 September.

Giele, J.Z. (1992) 'Promise and disappointment of the modern era: equality for women', in H. Kahne and J.Z. Giele (eds) *Women's Work and Women's Lives: The Continuing Struggle Worldwide*, Boulder, Co.: Westview Press.

Gora, M. (1991) 'Labour demand and labour supply in the period of transition', CEP working paper no. 130, London.

Heinen, J. (1994) 'The reintegration into work of unemployed women: issues and policies', in OECD, *Unemployment in Transition Countries: Transient or Persistent?* Paris: OECD.

Hochschild, A. (with A. Machung) (1989) *The Second Shift. Working Parents and the Revolution at Home*, New York: Viking.

ILO (1987) *World Labour Report 1987*, Geneva: ILO.

—— (1991) *Yearbook of Labour Statistics 1991*, Geneva: ILO.

—— (1992) *World Labour Report 1992*, Geneva: ILO.

—— (1995) *Yearbook of Labour Statistics 1995*, Geneva: ILO.

IMF (1994) *World Economic Outlook*, October, Washington DC: IMF.

Jankubowska, L. (1992) 'The dynamics of women's emancipation in Eastern Europe', Paper for workshop 'Agendas for women in Eastern and Western Europe', Centre for Women Studies, University of Nijmegen, 7 February.

Kornai, J. (1980) *Economics of Shortage*, vol. A–B, Amsterdam: North Holland.

OECD (1991) *Employment Outlook*, Paris: OECD.

—— (1992) *Reforming the Economies of Central and Eastern Europe*, Paris: OECD.

Paukert, L. (1991) 'The economic status of women in the transition to a market economy system: the case of Czechoslovakia', *International Labour Review*, 130(5/6), pp. 613–33.

Posadskaya, A. (1992) 'Bericht uit Moskou', *Tijdschrift voor Vrouwenstudies*, 13(4), pp. 492–6.

Rudolph, H., Appelbaum, E. and Maier, F. (1990) 'After German unity: a cloudier outlook for women', *Challenge*, 33(5), pp. 33–40.

Wheelock, J. (1990) *Husbands at Home: The Domestic Economy in a Post-Industrial Society*, London: Routledge.

Wolchik, S.L. (1992) 'Women and work in communist and post-communist Central and Eastern Europe', in H. Kahne and J.Z. Giele (eds) *Women's Work and Women's Lives: The Continuing Struggle Worldwide*, Boulder, Co.: Westview Press.

Women of Hungary (1991), Women of Europe (no. 32), Brussels: Commission of the European Communities.

Part III

POLICY
INSTRUMENTS

9

EQUAL OPPORTUNITIES IN THE EUROPEAN UNION: THEORY AND PRACTICE

Anneke van Doorne-Huiskes

INTRODUCTION

From the outset, the European Community and European Union have shown an interest in the equal treatment of women and men. In the 1950s this interest was primarily inspired by the fear of unfair competition between men and women, rather than any concern about the bad labour situation of women. Nevertheless, the European Union has become an important framework for equal opportunity policies in the member states.

This chapter provides an overview of policy measures developed in the European Community and European Union to strengthen the position of women on the labour market. First we start with a description of the directives, recommendations and action programmes formulated in recent decades. The third action programme was published in November 1990. Like the earlier programmes, it focuses on equal opportunities for men and women. An interesting point in this third action programme is its premise that efforts to improve the position of women on the labour market should no longer be seen as a separate policy item. The programme urges an integral approach, in which women's issues form part of a general labour market policy. This integrational approach will be continued in the recently launched Fourth Medium-Term Community Action Programme of Equal Opportunities for Women and Men (1996–2000).

Positive action can be considered a powerful instrument in a policy that aims to strengthen the position of women. So, in the following section, the positive action model is presented, as it has been developed in the European Union. A few examples of European companies in which positive action has been applied are also given.

It is not easy to effect greater equality between men and women on the labour market, largely because of inequalities in the area of unpaid labour. As long as unpaid childcare and household tasks are predominantly performed by women, their secondary position in the paid labour market will continue. This poses an interesting problem. Full participation of women in the labour market requires a redistribution of unpaid tasks and responsibilities among men and women. This involves a process of change which will not be easy, not only because men are rather unwilling in this respect, but also because the organization of paid labour is not geared to it. Therefore we emphasize that the actual creation of equal opportunities for women and men in the European Union requires a more flexible organization of labour, and other associated changes. A 'work–family fit' must be achieved in the labour market, as it were. A number of steps in this direction have already been made in Europe: the last section provides an evaluation of these measures and outlines some prospects for the future.

EQUAL OPPORTUNITIES IN THE EUROPEAN UNION: DIRECTIVES, RECOMMENDATIONS AND ACTION PROGRAMMES

The European Union has introduced various measures, all of which strive to effect a structure of equal opportunities for men and women. There are three types of measures, varying in the extent to which they are compulsorily imposed on member states: directives, recommendations and action programmes. A directive requires member states to alter national legislation within a defined period in order to comply with the content and tenor of the directive. Recommendations and action programmes aim at stimulating the establishment of policy in the individual member states. Besides directives, recommendations and action programmes, the EU has set up eleven networks, each with responsibilities for particular subjects throughout the union. They are called EU equality networks, and their creation is one of a series of practical measures designed to promote equality (Collins 1992).

Directives on equal opportunities

The European Community adopted six directives on equality of opportunity for men and women. The first was the Equal Pay Directive (75/117; 10 February 1975), which elaborates on the principle and implementation of equal pay for men and women, including the concept of 'equal pay for work of equal value'. This prohibits any discrimination on the basis of gender for equal labour or for labour to which equal value is attributed. The formulation 'work of equal value' is necessarily beset with pitfalls. The value attached to a job description is often determined on the basis of organization-specific job classification systems. Research in both the USA and the Netherlands suggests that such systems themselves are not always sexually neutral: chapter 10 in this volume goes into further details.

The second directive established the requirement of equal treatment of men and women (Directive 76/207; 9 February 1976). This Equal Treatment

140

Directive guarantees the principle of equal treatment in access to employment, vocational training and promotion. Equal treatment of men and women means that discrimination on the basis of gender, by directly or indirectly referring to civil status or family situation, is prohibited. This does not mean, however, that gender cannot in certain cases be a determining factor in access to a profession, and protective provisions with regard to pregnancy and motherhood are not ruled out by the principle of equal treatment.

The third directive (the Social Security Directive 79/17; 19 December 1979) relates to the progressive implementation of the principle of equal treatment for men and women in statutory social security systems. This concerns statutory regulations that provide protection against sickness, invalidity, old age, industrial accidents, unemployment and social welfare. In this case as well, every form of discrimination on the basis of gender, whether direct or indirect, is disallowed. The 1979 Social Security Directive was followed in 1986 by the Occupational Social Security Schemes Directive (86/378; 24 July 1986). This directive concerns social security legislation which is not covered under the third directive and which relates to employees and self-employed individuals from a particular group of companies, branches of industry or labour market sectors, such as pension plans for employees of a certain company or branch of industry.

The Self-Employment Directive was adopted in 1986 (86/613; 11 December). This directive relates to the extension of the principle of equal treatment to women who are employers or self-employed, or who work wholly or partly with their spouses. Finally, in 1992 (92/85; 19 October) the sixth directive on 'the protection of pregnant women at work, and those who have recently given birth or are breast-feeding their child' was adopted. This directive contains a number of minimum provisions, leaving it to the member states to adopt more favourable arrangements, with a non-regression clause to the effect that the level of protection currently in place must not be reduced.

The responsibility for monitoring legislation on equal pay, equal treatment in access to jobs, equal treatment for the self-employed, and the health and safety of pregnant workers is assigned to the European Commission's Equal Opportunities Unit. This Unit was set up in 1976, as part of Directorate-General V on Employment, Industrial Relations and Social Affairs. Monitoring legislation on the two social security directives is primarily the responsibility of the Social Security, Social Protection and Living Conditions Unit, also a part of DG V.

Recommendation on the promotion of positive action for women

The Recommendation on the Promotion of Positive Action for Women was adopted by the Council of the European Communities in December 1984. A recommendation imposes no compulsory requirements. It is a so-called flexible instrument, recommending that member states adopt a series of measures, policies or guidelines within a national framework. The 1984 recommendation appeals to member states to eliminate the disparities women experience in professional spheres through a positive action policy and to promote 'mixed' professions. This includes all policy initiatives that contribute to the elimination of unequal positions on the labour market, such as information campaigns, consciousness-raising activities and research in areas such as career guidance, the recruitment of women for higher positions, the active participation of women in decision-making bodies, and the division of paid and unpaid labour between men and women. Later, in the Council of Ministers, this positive action approach has come increasingly to be reserved for measures that directly relate to the position of women working in companies and organizations. This shift of focus from labour market issues in a more general context to the positions of women in companies and organizations will be further examined in the next section.

Action programmes

The action programmes are a significant part of the EU's equal opportunity policies. In an action programme, the EU itself provides resources and undertakes activities in order to promote a particular policy in member states. So far, four action programmes on equal opportunities for women and men have been successively launched, in the periods 1982–5, 1986–90, 1991–5, and 1996–2000.

The first action programme heavily stressed the legal obstacles standing in the way of equal opportunity for women, and the systematic augmentation of individual rights for women. These rights were to be achieved through compliance with and development of guidelines. Indirect discrimination was identified as a significant judicial principle in this connection. Indirect discrimination is unequal treatment on the basis of circumstances other than gender, because of which – nevertheless – persons of a particular gender are placed at a disadvantage. Indirect discrimination concerns the disadvantageous effect of measures or proceedings that, in practice, result in dissimilar treatment of men and women. Deliberate or intentional discrimination is not the issue in cases of indirect discrimination: the question is rather what actual result ensues from certain actions (see van Vleuten 1995). In addition to legal obstacles and measures, the first action programme also dealt with other impediments to equal opportunity for women, especially the influence of prejudices and their effects on the lasting segregation of men's and women's professions.

The second action programme called for more concrete policy. Initiatives had been taken on various issues, but concrete results were still necessary.

This was especially noticeable during periods in which women in particular, as a vulnerable category on the labour market, suffered from economic recession and unemployment. Accordingly, the second action programme urged an increase in women's participation in education and particularly a break from women's traditional educational choices. It also stated that equality in professional opportunity could only develop when there was greater equality of responsibility between men and women in the family. Childcare and parental leave provisions were included in this.

According to the third action programme, efforts to achieve a better labour market position for women should no longer be seen as a policy that is specific and limited in nature. 'Women's issues' are not isolated problems, but a component of more general problems on the labour market: 'The Third Action Programme provides for the integration of equality into general mainstream policy.' Equal opportunities should be integrated into the formulation and implementation of all relevant policies and action programmes at the EU and member state level. In a climate of increasing scarcity of trained labour, the EU cannot allow, according to the third action programme, the loss and under-utilization of women's potential. Women should be better integrated into the labour process, both in terms of numbers and quality. This requires more measures to increase opportunities for combining work outside the home with household duties. The action programme also advocated better application of existing laws in the area of equal treatment, and emphasized matters related to equal pay for work of equal value and indirect discrimination.

The fourth action programme (1996–2000) continues this integrational approach. Its overall aim is to promote integration of equal opportunities in the process of preparing, implementing and monitoring all policies, measures and activities at community, national, regional and local level. More specifically, initiatives are focused on equal opportunities in a changing economy, on encouraging a policy to reconcile family and working life for women and men, and on the promotion of a gender balance in decision-making.

THE EU MODEL OF POSITIVE ACTION

Reducing the impact of economic, social and cultural restrictions on the labour market positions and careers of women is one of the important aims of equal opportunity programmes in general and of positive action in a more specific sense. Positive action is to be considered as a policy instrument which tries to reduce and/or to relieve the various restrictions on women's career opportunities.

The main restriction of course is the division between paid and unpaid labour. Since women shoulder primary responsibility for unpaid household labour, they have to overcome more practical and moral opposition in order to achieve a career in the paid labour sector. This division of labour has resulted in institutions, regulations and procedures which, in their turn, increase the costs for women of investing in their own labour market position. For example, many tax systems and social security regulations favour households consisting of breadwinners and economically dependent partners over two-income couples.

Structures and cultures have also arisen at the level of organizations, which make the choice for a career more complicated and therefore more costly for women than for men. For example, Moss Kanter (1977) has pointed to opportunity structures and the existence of dead-end jobs. The cultures of organizations are also important as regards the question of whether women have as many promotion possibilities as men. Preconceptions about women are not uncommon, especially when women have only a token presence in a department or company. Women, more than men, have to deal with a reversed onus of proof in organizations. It could be said that credibility is generally ascribed to men, until proven otherwise, while women have to create credibility in the face of initial attitudes of suspicion and scepticism.

Reducing these economic, social and cultural restrictions is a far from simple process. These are more than just a few coincidental characteristics that are easily altered. On the contrary, equal opportunity policies are geared to the core institutional and cultural characteristics of organizations, characteristics which in their turn are firmly rooted in the structure and culture of Western society.

From a broad concept to a more restricted one

Initially, the European Commission employed a broad notion of positive action (see de Jong and Bock 1995), including not only information and the raising of public awareness but also the diversification of career options through education and the stimulation of measures that would lead to a more balanced distribution of paid and unpaid labour between men and women. Later the term positive action was increasingly reserved for measures directly involved with women's positions in companies and organizations. In the positive action handbook that the Commission issued in 1988, the positive action programme was seen as 'a comprehensive planning process which an employer chooses to undertake in order to achieve a more balanced representation of women and men throughout the organization's work force'. 'In essence', the handbook states,

> positive action is part of overall human resources planning. The setting up of a positive action programme in general includes four stages: a commitment stage, in which the organization announces its commitment to positive action; an analysis stage, in which all relevant

data concerning the organization's work force and employment practices are collected and analysed; a planning stage, in which the programme is worked out in detail for future implementation; [and] an implementation stage, in which the programme and a system to monitor outcomes are set in motion.

(Commission of the European Communities, 1988)

The European Commission based this description of a positive action programme on the model of affirmative action which was developed in the USA in the 1970s. The emphasis on management's responsibility for positive action policy was adopted in the European concept, as was an analysis of personnel figures, the recording of results, and regular evaluation of progress. The EU positive action concept, like its American precursor, also indicated that this involves flexible instruments that can be applied in specific company situations. However, a significant difference between the EU positive action concept and the affirmative action model was the lack of reference to proportional representation of women and men as an objective of policy efforts. In the US, the setting of numerical quotas has always been heavily emphasized (see de Jong and Bock 1995). Members of the European Commission did not wish to adopt that powerful element of equal opportunity policy, not because they considered these instruments inefficient, but rather for political reasons. Even the European civil servants of the Equal Opportunities Unit, who were in charge of designing positive action proposals, were convinced that setting numerical quotas would be a politically unrealistic option, if not for the members of the European Committee, then certainly for the Council of Ministers.

With this decision, the potential power of positive action as an EU instrument to improve women's status in the European labour force was severely weakened from the outset. Apart from the law on equal opportunity, which applies to all member states, no monitoring mechanisms have been developed at the level of the European Union to assess the position of women. In fact, the national governments of the EU have a decisive say in what is going on in relation to women's issues in their own countries. This national dominance will certainly continue in the coming years. For women, the consequences will almost certainly be negative. In a climate of economic deterioration and increasing unemployment, national governments tend to be reluctant to spend extra money on women's issues. Setting up specific arrangements in favour of women is increasingly considered to be the responsibility of the 'social partners' (unions and employers), although there are different traditions in the different member states. This means that women's issues must be defended in the negotiations between trade unions and employers. This shifts the problem to an arena in which women are poorly represented (Outshoorn 1991, Krug in this volume).

Positive action in daily practice

As a consequence of this lack of European coherence on positive action, its daily practice in organizations is varied. For example, a law went into force in Italy in 1991 aiming at achieving equality of men and women in the labour process. Every company with more than 100 employees has to submit a report every two years to trade unions and regional political authorities on the situation of women and men in the company.

In Belgium, the government has concluded central agreements with the business community, in which resolutions have been adopted to make arrangements for positive action in the various professional sectors. In 1987 a Royal Decree on positive action was adopted, which is applicable in the private sector. Positive actions are conducted in the form of equal opportunity schemes, comprising either measures to correct the adverse effects of traditional social situations and behaviour patterns for women, or measures to promote the presence and participation of women in professional life in all occupational sectors and at all levels of the hierarchy (Vogel-Polsky 1989). What is important in the context of this chapter is that adoption of an equal opportunity scheme in the private sector in Belgium is entirely optional. This does not mean, however, that nothing happens. Some interesting initiatives have been developed in large banks, one of which has set a target figure of 33 per cent for the proportion of women among the young trainees it recruits. Philips of Belgium has also established a quota for the recruitment of young women graduates. Other companies have developed training programmes for personnel managers on the integration of positive action in human resources management, along with training programmes for female workers on career development, assertiveness and so on (Chalude et al. 1994). In the public sector the situation of women has to be evaluated annually, in a report to the national government.

In France, equal opportunity objectives can be either integrated in collective agreements or initiated by Works Councils within firms. The 1983 law on professional equality forms the legal basis for positive actions. Each year, companies have to draw up a report on the status of women in comparison to men in the fields of recruitment, training, promotion, qualification, working conditions and pay. This report must be discussed with the members of the Works Councils (Chalude et al. 1994). This obligation also applies to the public sector.

As in other countries, specific policies for women are hard to justify in France at the moment, due to a declining economy and rising unemployment rates. More emphasis is given to the general development of human resources, as a key factor for improved business performance. Nevertheless, action schemes in firms have helped women to develop their careers, and have extended the tasks of secretaries and given them better prospects for promotion to managerial jobs. For unskilled and semi-skilled workers, including women, some firms have designed courses on economics, banking and communication. These courses might give them access to better jobs in the near future.

The Netherlands has an incentive regulation favouring positive action in the private sector, but this has not yet produced the desired results. A 1990 survey of a sample of 842 organizations with over 100 employees showed that only 4 per cent had a positive action plan with a coherent set of measures (Chalude et al. 1994). In the public sector, targets have been set for women's representation: 20 per cent women in the higher ranks in 1995 and an average of 30 per cent women in public administration. Action schemes have been developed to meet these targets, including part-time opportunities (32–hour working weeks) in senior positions, management courses specifically for women, and the reservation of some functions for female candidates, if underrepresentation is evident.

Denmark is the only country in the EU in which an employers' organization (DA) has provided financial support for positive action. Approximately 1.5 million crowns are available through the DA for projects whose purpose is to increase the number of women in non-traditional professions (de Jong and Bock 1995).

At the business sector level, positive action initiatives in the EU have become common in banks and television companies. For example, the equal opportunity policies in large banks in the UK and the Netherlands appear to be relatively well-developed, including re-entry programmes for employees who leave the bank temporarily to care for children, management training centred on the theme of equal opportunity, career training for women, the screening of selection procedures to remove any conscious or unconscious discrimination on the basis of gender, and target figures for the recruitment of young women college and university graduates for bank positions. In the Netherlands, an equal opportunities protocol was incorporated in a bank's Collective Labour Agreement for the first time in 1990 (de Jong and Bock 1995). This protocol provided guidelines for an active equal opportunity policy to increase the recruitment of women, enhance their promotion opportunities, provide training facilities, implement measures against sexual harassment, offer childcare facilities and parental leave, and increase the possibility of part-time work.

Positive action; motivating factors and obstacles

Because of the specific European approach to positive action, without a statutory reference to the proportional representation of women and men as an objective of policy efforts, European experiences with positive action reveal some factors that prompt its implementation and others that do not (Positive Action Network 1992). The main motivating factor appears to be the contribution a positive action scheme can make to the better

147

management of human resources as an integral part of company strategy. Thus, in order to maximize its chances of success, a positive action scheme must be presented as an aspect of a strategy for change in organizational development and in the development of human resources. Designing positive action programmes as a strategy to bring together the company's development and the professional development of women turns out to be one of the greatest factors for success. In this integrated approach, commitment from company management is a key factor in any decision to adopt a positive action programme. Genuine, visible, top-level commitment does motivate others to take positive action seriously and to consider it as an important management tool to raise the firm's performance.

Another motivating factor may be the shortage of well-trained workers, due for instance to rapid changes in technology. If, in such a situation, low-skilled women are available, training programmes will be developed and women will be given access to traditionally male-dominated areas. Demographic arguments, indicating a decreasing number of young people entering the labour market, sometimes prove to be a supportive factor for positive action schemes, although this only holds if the effects of demographic developments are already visible in daily practice.

The main obstacles to implementing positive action programmes arise where companies, particularly in times of economic downturn or crisis, adopt a conservative attitude and do not take any measures which, in their opinion, constitute a risk. Positive action schemes may then be seen as unnecessary expenses. Often, companies fear far-reaching changes in the organization of work. Other obstacles arise from a lack of financial incentives for positive action, the lack of a framework to maintain momentum, or a lack of enthusiasm or persuasiveness from management. In general, it is not easy to sustain interest in positive action schemes, and to keep them vigorous and at the centre of organizational activity, after the first cycle of activity.

THE NECESSITY OF A 'WORK–FAMILY FIT'

Although positive action initiatives are under way in various parts of Europe, figures on the situation of women in the labour market at national and European levels show only very gradual improvement. The causes of this slow progress lie in economic circumstances, the lack of instruments to enforce implementation, a lack of political will to give high priority to improving women's status in society, and deeply rooted structural and cultural characteristics in all European societies. One of the largest problems is the disparity between men and women in the area of unpaid labour (see Plantenga in this volume). Women do much more work in addition to their paid labour, a fact which sustains the structural inequality between women and men. This structural inequality is in fact beyond the scope of positive action as an equal opportunity instrument, since it is primarily focused at the level of organizations.

In the publication *Shaping Structural Change: The Role of Women*, the Organization for Economic Co-operation and Development (OECD) speaks of an implicit 'social contract' in its argument for an 'active society' (OECD 1994). This social contract has two components, the gender contract and the employment contract. Both these contracts define the current division of family and labour market roles. In the gender contract, women assume the bulk of family care and domestic functions, while men are assigned primary responsibility for the family's economic or financial well-being. This social contract conflicts with the new reality of men's and women's lives. Double-income and single-adult families are increasingly common, while households with full-time home-makers have declined dramatically. Most women are now forced to juggle household and family demands with involvement in paid work structures that are designed to fit male employment patterns. As the OECD report states, men miss out on the emotional rewards of the care and development of children, because they are similarly constrained by the gender-based division of household and employment responsibilities. The acknowledgment of women as principal economic actors is an interesting element of the OECD report. Women are not a burden on the economy. On the contrary, the solution to economic problems depends on the enhancement of women's economic role. According to *Shaping Structural Change*, women are a key resource that is currently under-utilized, both quantitatively and qualitatively.

On the basis of this view of women's labour, the OECD advocates increased compatibility between employment and family responsibilities. This process requires cultural changes as well as alterations in the social infrastructure, which must be achieved through both public and private provisions. The OECD underlines that employers benefit from better compatibility between employment and family responsibilities. Pay-offs for employers range from reduced absenteeism, decreased staff turnover and savings on concomitant recruitment costs, to an enhanced corporate reputation. Family responsibilities, however, are not limited merely to caring for children. Demands for care and services for the growing number of elderly people also need to be urgently addressed, according to the OECD.

The EC and EU have been giving attention to the reconciliation of employment and family responsibilities for quite some time. In 1983, the Commission proposed a Directive on Parental Leave, an initiative which was, however, blocked by the Council of Ministers of that time. Not until the spring of 1992 did the Council of Ministers adopt the Recommendation on Childcare as part of the third Equal Opportunity Programme and the Action Programme to implement the Social Charter. As mentioned earlier, in October 1992 the Council of Ministers adopted a directive on the protection of pregnant women at work. Pregnant women may not be dismissed for reasons connected with their condition. Another minimum provision in the directive is obligatory maternity leave of 14 uninterrupted weeks. In most countries, maternity leave exceeds 14 weeks: the range goes from 13 weeks in Portugal to 28 weeks in Denmark, the median being 16 weeks.

But the socio-political debate on the reconciliation of employment and work embraces other issues, such as childcare, career interruptions, and equity or equality of opportunity within the family and in the labour market (Dumon 1992). In relation to the labour market, a study carried out under the auspices of the European Commission sought examples of family-friendly employers in Europe (Hogg and Harker 1992). It included twenty-five companies from seven EU countries that have developed work–family arrangements. These arrangements vary in nature, ranging from flexitime, part-time work, flexiplace and teleworking, family leave, childcare support, adult care support, information and referral services, and career break programmes. These measures are often incorporated in a more general equal opportunities policy. The Danish State Railways are a good example. An equal opportunity programme has been in progress there since 1987, at a cost to the employer of 1 million crowns (more than 125,000 ECUs) per year. This programme includes not only work–family issues, but also training programmes for women in management, programmes to recruit women for male-dominated professions, and workshops to improve gender relations at all levels in the workplace.

DISCUSSION

If all the various initiatives in progress in the EU in the area of equal opportunities for women and men are considered in terms of results, things do not appear to be changing very rapidly. It takes a long time to eliminate old structures and cultural attitudes and to create a new relationship between men and women on the European labour market. One of the main obstacles in this process is the disparity between men and women in the area of unpaid work. If this disparity is not solved, inequalities between women and men will not disappear. The Green Paper on European social policy, presented by the European Commission at the end of 1993, speaks of making better use of the talents of women and developing a more balanced society. Three main issues are mentioned in relation to this concept of a more balanced society: the reconciliation of employment and family responsibilities, the vertical and horizontal desegregation of the labour market, and an increase in women's participation in decision-making.

It is not difficult to list the prerequisites for a balanced society, but the question of how these measures are to be settled in such a way that the programmes will really be carried out is much more complicated. One suggestion in the Green Paper is to use specific goals and timetables, including quotas, targets and positive measures, to ensure the fuller participation of women in areas in which they are underrepresented. Another suggestion is to develop monitoring mechanisms to assess continually the positions of women, not only in relation to representation, but also in relation to family-friendly policies and the organization of working time.

At what level, if at all, it will be possible to develop monitoring systems in this sense is an interesting question. At the level of the European Union itself, this seems to be a very unrealistic option for the moment. The member states have to cope with high unemployment rates and, in the short term, all are reluctant to create specific measures and monitoring systems for women. In the longer term however, the development of all of the talent in the European Union, of males as well as of females, is very important. The continuation and development of a quality-based production system requires that investment in people be given the highest priority, not only for economic reasons, but – in the European tradition – for political and social reasons as well. Workers have to have and to keep the right to education and training opportunities, and they need to be in touch with the processes of change which are going on and will continue in all European firms and enterprises. Besides this, acceptable standards of social security have to be guaranteed. We face the challenging question of how, in the next century, an acceptable social security system will be defined. Individual responsibility will inevitably form a major part of it, but individual responsibilities can only be developed if all people, men as well as women, have access to opportunities on the labour market and in family life.

REFERENCES

Chalude, M., Jong, A. de and Laufer, J. (1994) 'Implementing equal opportunity and affirmative action programmes in Belgium, France and The Netherlands', in M.J. Davidson and R.J. Burk (eds) *Women in Management, Current Research Issues*, London: Paul Chapman.

Collins, H. (1992) *The Equal Opportunities Handbook*, Oxford/Cambridge, Mass.: Blackwell Publishers.

Dumon, W. (1992) *National Family Policies in EC Countries in 1991*, DG V, Brussels: Commission of the European Communities.

Green Paper (1993) *Green Paper – European Social Policy. Options for the Union*, DG V, Luxembourg: Office for Official Publications of the European Communities.

Hogg, Chr. and Harker, L. (1992) *The Family-Friendly Employer: Examples from Europe*, London: Daycare Trust.

Jong, A.M. de and Bock, B. (1995) 'Positive action in organizations within the European Union', in A. van Doorne-Huiskes, J. van Hoof, and E. Roelofs (eds) *Women and the European Labour Markets*, London: Paul Chapman.

Moss Kanter, R. (1977) *Men and Women of the Corporation*, New York: Basic Books.

OECD (1994) 'Shaping Structural Change: The Role of Women', in OECD, *Women and Structural Change: New Perspectives*, Paris: OECD.

Outshoorn, J. (1991) 'Is this what we wanted? Positive action as issue perversion', in E. Meehan and S. Sevenhuijsen, *Equality Politics and Gender*, London: Sage.

Positive Action Network (1992) *Motivating Factors, Obstacles and Guidelines*, Equal Opportunities Unit – DG V, Brussels: Commission of the European Communities.

Vleuten, T. van (1995) 'Legal instrument at the EU level', in A. van Doorne-Huiskes, J. van Hoof and E. Roelofs (eds) *Women and the European Labour Markets*, London: Paul Chapman.

Vogel-Polsky, E. (1989) *Positive Action and the Constitutional and Legislative Hindrances to its Implementation in the Member States of the Council of Europe*, European Committee for Equality between Women and Men, Strasburg: Council of Europe.

10

COMPARABLE WORTH AND EQUAL PAY POLICIES IN THE EUROPEAN UNION

Jeanne de Bruijn

INTRODUCTION

Comparable worth, or pay equity, is a concept used in equal pay strategies, mostly in the US and Canada, where the comparable worth movement emerged at the end of the 1970s. The core postulate behind comparable worth or pay equity is that jobs performed by women offer lower wages than jobs of comparable value that are performed by men. Comparable worth or pay equity thus refers to a type of discrimination that occurs when the sex composition of jobs has a net effect on their wages. This sort of discrimination can only occur where jobs are substantially segregated by sex, a condition which is generally the case.

A fair system of job evaluation is an important instrument to establish scientifically the comparable worth of female and male jobs. This chapter therefore starts with a short overview of the different approaches taken so far towards the persistent wage inequality between men and women. The next section concentrates on job evaluation systems, as an instrument for measuring comparable worth and as an instrument with a gender subtext. Subsequently, the juridical possibilities of the struggle for equal pay are explored, while the last section deals with future strategies.

THE STRUGGLE FOR EQUAL PAY

The international recognition of the principle of equal pay for men and women dates from the establishment of the International Labour Organization in 1919, which incorporates this principle in its constitution. The Universal Declaration of Human Rights in 1948 embraced this principle as well. Article 119 of the Treaty of Rome of 1958, the foundation document of the European Community, states that 'Member States ensure and subsequently maintain the application of the principle that men and women should receive equal pay for equal work'. Member states at that time were apparently unwilling to adopt the wider concept of equal pay for work of equal value which was the standard of the ILO Convention 100 (ILO

1951). It was 1975 before the European Council of Ministers issued a directive on the issue of equal pay. This 'Council Directive of 10 February 1975 on the approximation of the laws of the Member States relating to the application of the principle of equal pay for men and women' (75/117/EEC) signalled the start for legislation on equal pay for work of equal value in all member states. This directive states, in article 1, that

> The principle of equal pay for men and women outlined in Article 119 of the Treaty, hereinafter called the 'principle of equal pay', means, for the same work or for the work to which equal value is attributed, the elimination of all discrimination on grounds of sex with regard to all aspects and conditions of remuneration. In particular, where a job classification system is used for determining pay, it must be based on the same criteria for both men and women and so drawn up as to exclude any discrimination on ground of sex.
>
> (*Official Journal of the European Communities*, 19–2–75, No. L 45/19)

Despite this growing legislation, the wage gap between men and women has proved to be very persistent. Almost twenty years after the first directive, pay differentials between men and women still exist in all countries of the European Community, although to a slightly varying extent (Bellace 1988, Rubery 1991). Figures of the OECD (1991) indicate that, in Western industrialized countries, the gross hourly wages of women are on average 70–75 per cent of those of men. Even wider differences in rewards could be found if pay data also included access to fringe benefits.

The stability of the wage differences between men and women has stimulated various research (Plantenga and van Velzen 1993: 6–9). Among economists, the human capital theory has been rather popular. In this approach, wage differences between men and women are reduced to differences in productivity as a consequence of differences in training and experience. For all manner of reasons, women have invested less in human capital and the result is that they are less productive than men and therefore earn less. Women have invested less in human capital, for example, because it is assumed that they will interrupt their working life at some time and therefore the investment in a specific training course will not produce sufficient returns.

This theory was especially popular in the 1970s and 1980s, and explains the strong focus on education and training in that period. In the middle of the 1990s, women are hardly lagging behind in training if this is measured in years of schooling and training. However, differences in years of experience still exist; women work part-time far more often than men and their careers are interrupted more frequently than men's. According to Treiman and Hartmann (1981) human capital factors explain at most 50 per cent of the wage gap between the sexes. This leads to the conclusion that education and training may be important in explaining wage differences, but other factors apparently also play a role.

The human capital theory's failure to explain adequately wage differences has stimulated the search for other potential causes. In the 1980s, great emphasis was placed on the fact that, in spite of their almost equal qualifications, men and women were distributed very differently over professions and jobs. In other words, great attention was paid to horizontal and vertical occupational segregation. In this segregation approach, the assumption is that the extent of occupational segregation indicates that women are recruited and selected for very specific jobs and positions. These jobs and positions generally offer not only low average wages, but also limited career prospects. They are often dead-end jobs, without opportunities for internal promotion. According to the segregation theory, this imbalanced distribution of women and men over professions and job levels largely determines the difference in pay between men and women. In order to close the pay gap, employers' recruitment and promotion policies are highlighted and attempts are made to achieve a fairer distribution of men and women at the various job levels through affirmative action programmes.

At the end of the 1980s, however, more and more questions were being raised about the effectiveness of this strategy, and especially on the necessity of breaking down horizontal occupation segregation. The anti-segregation strategy was seen to have been one-sided because the responsibility for its abolition was placed almost exclusively on women themselves. In addition, the emphasis on technical occupations was perceived as undervaluing those caring professions traditionally associated with women and femininity. Thus, the focus shifted to the question of why jobs performed primarily by women systematically receive lower pay than those performed predominantly by men. Why does a child-minder earn less than a traffic warden, a kindergarten teacher less than an animal keeper, a nurse less than a police officer, and a midwife less than a hotel clerk? Why couldn't women's pay be changed to such an extent that, even given extensive horizontal occupational segregation, women and men earned about the same?

In this 'institutional' approach (Plantenga and van Velzen 1993: 9) interest was focused especially on the question how pay is determined. For example, it is conceivable that the wage stipulations in collective labour agreements (CLA) do not apply to the same extent to female and male employees. Inequality could be the result of the exclusion of certain jobs, especially those performed primarily by women, from the CLA, or the exclusion of certain employment contracts, especially those entered into with female employees. Where the CLA does apply, it is possible that stipulations on pay do not always result in equal wages for equal or equivalent work. This latter variation has stimulated research on job-evaluation systems (e.g., Treiman and Hartmann 1981, England 1992, Evans and Nelson 1989, Acker 1989). The essential difference between the human capital and institutional approach is that, in the latter, wage differences are no longer attributed to individual characteristics of men and women, but to differences in the evaluation of specific jobs – a situation which the segregation approach had also indicated. But whereas the segregation approach aspires to redistribute men and women over occupations and sectors, the institutional approach is primarily aimed at changing the wages of occupations.

JOB EVALUATION

Given the importance attached to job evaluation systems in recent research on wage differences between men and women, some extra information on this new instrument seems necessary. In principle, job evaluation makes it possible to compare jobs throughout the organization, the economic sector or even in the entire economy. This is an important precondition in the struggle for equal pay, as the extent of occupational segregation often makes it difficult to make a comparison between a man and a woman doing different work, but work of more or less the same value. In such cases, job evaluation can answer the question of whether both do work of equal value. If a woman's job has been graded the same as a man's job under a job evaluation system, in principle, in most countries in the EU, the Equal Pay Act gives the right to claim the same wage.

There are three main types of job evaluation systems: the ranking method, the comparative or classification method and the analytical method. The analytical method is the most widely used, and involves analysing jobs into factors which are quantified according to a scale. 'Points rating', for example, is an analytical method of job evaluation widely used in the Netherlands. Under this method, jobs are broken down into different factors, e.g. knowledge, responsibility and working conditions.[1] Factors are often divided into sub-factors. The factors are awarded points according to a predetermined scale, and the total of points determines a job's place in the ranking order. Factors are usually weighted to reflect the varying degrees of importance attached to each. Job evaluation can be used for a number of organizational goals. One is to rank jobs and to provide a basis for a grading and pay structure within organizations. The essence of such an evaluation process is that qualitative requirements for jobs are translated into quantitative units (points), and ultimately into a salary structure (de Bruijn 1991).

Of course, job evaluation systems are supposed to be objective and gender-neutral. The aim is to evaluate the job, not the job holder. It is recognized, however, that to some extent any assessment of a job's total demands relative to another will always contain some subjective elements.

Moreover, job evaluation is in large part a social procedure, establishing agreed differences within organizations, sometimes with a long history. In this respect, tracing the gender subtext of the evaluation systems is important, i.e. making visible the underlying, often implicit and 'natural' meanings of maleness and femaleness contained in neutral-looking rules and procedures, and tracing the effects of these subtexts in shaping hierarchical gender relations. Therefore, the unravelling of job evaluation systems, tracing the gender subtext, and tracing the options and decisions of the relevant agents in the process, may be important steps in revealing the more hidden dimensions of the pay differences between men and women.

There are several ways in which the job evaluation system results in wage differences to the detriment of women. The job descriptions may be incomplete, the application of the job evaluation system may be discriminatory, and the system of job evaluation may be biased. Research so far has shown the incompleteness of job descriptions of women's jobs. Research in various countries (e.g. the US, UK, Australia and the Netherlands) has shown that typical characteristics of women's jobs, such as caring and social skills, are usually omitted in job evaluation systems (Remick 1984, Bajema 1989, and for an overview see Jones 1993). Other research shows gendered application of systems. For example, when a system for defining comparable male and female jobs was applied by job evaluators who were aware of possible gender bias, the results were different from those obtained in the original application of the system, by evaluators who were not conscious of the gender issue (LTD 1988, Veldman and Wittink 1990, van Stigt 1994).

Dutch research has also shown a skewed gender structure in the systematics and dynamics of the system (Herik and Janssen 1991, Bajema 1991, de Bruijn et al. 1992). The logic of the system means that women's occupations will appear to be less valued than men's. When a job requires a low level of knowledge, for example, it is also assumed to have a low level of responsibility. The system's guidelines do not allow for a higher grading. However, in a number of women's jobs, a low level of knowledge is combined with a high level of responsibility, for instance among day-care workers or geriatric aides. The system of job evaluation may also be discriminatory in the sense that factors may be assigned different grades when applied to typical characteristics of male or of female work. For example, there are several indications that heavy physical work such as lifting and carrying objects scores higher on the factor 'physical effort' than lifting and carrying people, be they elderly, handicapped, or very young. Lifting an elderly person who weighs 75 kilos in and out of bed six times a day is caring work, women's work, and therefore not valued as heavy work. In more general terms, it appears that the physical effort in women's jobs is easily overlooked. The same applies to 'dirty work': oil, mud, smells, poisons, etc. are more readily observed than human vomit, blood, faeces, etc. Similarly, 'repetitive movements in the work' (i.e., manual dexterity and skill) is less likely to be recorded as physical effort than occasional heavy lifting, and under the heading 'execution of numerous tasks simultaneously', solving different mental tasks/problems at the same time is more readily observed as a complex function than carrying out numerous practical tasks at the same time, as is the case in many women's jobs such as those of secretary, nurse or primary school teacher. A last example of the sex bias of job evaluation systems refers to the fact that some factors may be described differently for women's and men's jobs. In the health-care sector, for example, the factor 'contacts' in men's jobs is perceived as contacts with colleagues, contacts linked to work and the organization. For women's jobs, however, this is described as contacts with patients, i.e. at the level of carrying out nursing and caring tasks.

EQUAL VALUE, INDIRECT DISCRIMINATION AND THE LAW

The reconstruction of the gender subtext in the process of job evaluation can explain some of the persistence of wage differences between men and women. The question remains of how this new approach can be used in the struggle for equal pay. What are the juridical experiences so far?

The first EC directive requires equal pay for work of equal value. Thus far, however, the legal possibilities in cases of equal pay for men's and women's work are relatively unexplored (Boelens and Veldman 1993). The concept of equal value, for example, has been interpreted in most countries as more or less synonymous with equal work. As a result there are relatively few cases clarifying the concept of equal value. There is also little jurisprudence on the concepts of job evaluation and indirect discrimination, so far.

With regard to job evaluation systems, there is little awareness in the business world of the European Union that systems of job evaluation – official ones or more informal ones – do fall under the first EC directive, or that this directive has the status of law in the member states. Managers often think that the choice and use of job evaluation systems is the concern only of management; they buy or hire a system from a consultancy firm and introduce it, perhaps in consultation with their employees. However, job evaluation systems are not only instruments for setting wage structures; they are also instruments of proof in cases of unequal pay for work of equal value. So there are certain quality standards which a fair job evaluation system must meet. The European Court has formulated the criterion that the characteristics of male jobs in a job evaluation system have to be compensated by characteristics of female jobs. In other words, the job evaluation system must be balanced in this respect. Furthermore, there are some statements of the European Court in cases submitted by member states. The most interesting one is the Danfoss case from Denmark. The European Court stated that when a wage system is completely lacking in transparency, it is incumbent on the employer to prove that the pay for males and females does not infringe the Equal Pay Act. In premise 16 it reads

> The Equal Pay Directive must be interpreted as meaning that where an undertaking applies a system of pay which is totally lacking in transparency, it is for the employer to prove that his practice in the matter of wages is not discriminatory, if a female worker establishes, in relation to a relatively large number of employees, that the average pay for women is less than that for men.
>
> (ECR 1989)

Despite these scattered statements of the Court, not much has been laid down so far about the quality requirements of a fair job evaluation system.

Another concept which needs more clarification is that of indirect discrimination. Cases brought to court so far generally deal with the concept of direct discrimination, since they seek to obtain equal pay for equal work. When it comes to equal pay for work of equal value, however, indirect discrimination is involved: the problem is not a direct gender difference but a difference in the valuation of so-called male or female jobs. Indirect discrimination is expressly outlawed by the Equal Treatment Directive (76/207/EEC), which states that 'The principle of equal treatment shall mean that there shall be no discrimination whatsoever on grounds of sex either directly or indirectly by reference in particular to marital or family status' (Social Europe 1991: 38). While there is no explicit definition of indirect discrimination contained in the Equal Treatment Directive, the European Court has clarified this concept through its jurisprudence (in the case of Bilka-Kaufhaus Gmbh v. von Hartz). The Court held in this case that a practice which excluded part-time workers, where the exclusion affects a far greater proportion of women than men, was unlawful unless the employer could provide objective justification for the practice, unrelated to any discrimination on grounds of sex.

The Commission has attempted to provide a clear definition of the concept of indirect discrimination in its proposals for a Council Directive on the burden of proof in the area of equal pay and equal treatment for women and men. The proposed formulation is that

> indirect discrimination exists where an apparently neutral provision, criterion or practice disproportionately disadvantages the members of one sex, by reference in particular to marital or family status, and is not objectively justified by any necessary reason or condition unrelated to the sex of the person in question.
>
> (ibid.)

The purpose of including such a definition was to help complainants, employers, national courts and tribunals to understand and apply the concept better, thus contributing to the effective application of national laws which implement Community law. However, this directive was blocked in the Council of Ministers at the end of 1988 and discussions have yet to be revived by the Council.

FURTHER STRATEGIES

When it comes to further strategies, the intention of the Equal Opportunities Unit (EOU) to develop a Memorandum to reinforce the effects of the Equal Pay Directive, by prescribing more detailed policies for member states, is an important step in the right direction. A comparative study of all juridical and social aspects of 'equal pay for work of equal value' is the background for this Memorandum. Part of the Memorandum will be about the meaning of 'equal value' and about the role job evaluation could play in it. Further statements on the quality standards of job evaluation systems can be expected in the near future, either in European policy or in collective bargaining agreements.

Given this situation, a dual strategy seems necessary. On the one hand more jurisprudence on the concepts of 'equal value', 'indirect discrimination' and on the burden of proof seems essential. But to avoid a long line of endless court cases, it is also necessary to stipulate in collective agreements that job evaluation schemes and other wage structure practices which are used will be screened for gender bias and transparency. It will therefore be necessary for employers or consultancy firms to have their systems screened by independent and qualified researchers. Otherwise, judges and attorneys shall have to become job evaluation experts.

In the long run, non-discriminatory job evaluation should lead to a payment system within which work of equal value receives equal pay regardless of sex. As this will definitely improve the position of women on the labour market, a commitment to fair job evaluation systems may be considered as a second policy line, alongside an affirmative action policy. The two policies are in some sense complementary. Affirmative action is directed more at women with career aspirations or with aspirations to hold male jobs. Comparable worth addresses the biggest part of the female labour force: those who work in female jobs. Affirmative action attacks the skewed allocation of jobs over the sexes, comparable worth attacks the allocation of salaries over jobs predominantly held by men or predominantly by women. Affirmative action is a more person-oriented approach, directed at improving individual upward mobility, whereas comparable worth is directed at groups of people in the same job, to achieve collective upward mobility of the job. Affirmative action is also logically different from comparable worth, because affirmative action is directed to *persons*, male

160

and female. Comparable worth operates on the *occupational* rather than the individual level. Therefore it is an indirect way to attack discrimination on the basis of gender. Comparable worth leads to new strategies in weakening the sex segregation on the labour market, not by reallocating males and females over jobs (as via affirmative action), but by revaluing jobs to show that the values of men's and women's jobs are less unequal than the wage gap suggests.

NOTES

1　In the US and Canada the law establishes the factors on which jobs have to be compared, but this is not the case in the EU.

REFERENCES

Acker, J. (1989) *Doing Comparable Worth. Gender, Class and Pay Equity*, Philadelphia: Temple University Press.

Armstrong, P. and Armstrong, H. (1990) 'Lessons from pay equity', *Studies in Political Economy*, 32(2), pp. 29–54.

Bajema, C. (1989) *Functiebeschrijvingen Kritisch Bekeken*, Groningen: Rijksuniversiteit Groningen.

—— (1991) *Onderscheid naar Sekse bij Functiewaardering* (onderzoeksrapport ten behoeve van het FNV Vrouwensecretariaat en de Dienstenbond FNV), Rijksuniversiteit Groningen: Projectgroep Vrouwenarbeid; Vrije Universiteit Amsterdam: Sectie Beleid, Cultuur en Seksevraagstukken.

Bellace, J.R. (1988) 'A foreign perspective', in E.R. Livernash (ed.) *Comparable Worth: Issues and Alternatives*, Washington DC: Equal Employment Advisory Council.

Boelens, L. and Veldman, A.G. (1993) *Gelijkwaardige Arbeid, Gelijk Gewaardeerd*, Utrecht: Ministerie van Sociale Zaken en Werkgelegenheid.

—— (1991) 'Functiewaardering en de beloning van vrouwenwerk', *Tijdschrift voor Vrouwenstudies*, 12(1), pp. 19–31.

Bruijn, J. de, Bajema, C. and Timmerman, G. (1992) 'Indirecte discriminatie in functiewaardering', *Nemesis*, 8(5), pp. 21–9.

Commission of the European Communities (1988) *Report on the Implementation of the Promotion of Positive Action for Women 13 December 1984* (Com 88-370), Brussels.

ECR (1989) *European Court Reports*, Case 109/88, Handels-OG Kantorfunctionaerernes Forbund i Danmark v. Dansk Arbejdsgiverforening, ECR, p. 3199.

England, P. (1992) *Comparable Worth: Theories and Evidence*, New York: De Gruyter.

Evans, S. and Nelson, B. (1989) *Wage Justice. Comparable Worth and the Paradox of Technocratic Reform*, Chicago/London: University of Chicago Press.

Herik, C. van den and Janssen, U. (1991) *Functiewaardering en Sekse-onderscheid in de Gezondheidszorg*, Amsterdam/Zoetermeer: Vrije Universiteit/AbvaKabo.

ILO (1951) *International Labour Organization's Convention No. 100 on Equal Remuneration for Men and Women Workers*, Geneva: ILO.

Jones, B. (1993) 'Assessing equal work and work of equal value', discussion paper for the Seminar 'Equal Pay, 36 Years Later: in Search of Excellence?!', Equal Opportunity Unit – DG V, 25–26 October, Brussels.

LTD (Loontechnische Dienst) (1988) *Toepassing Bedrijfstakgebonden Functiewaarderingsregelingen in Nederland*, Ministerie van Sociale Zaken en Werkgelegenheid, 's-Gravenhage: SDU.

NCPE (National Committee on Pay Equity) (1989) *Pay Equity Activity in the Public Sector, 1979–1989*, Washington DC.

OECD (1991) *Equal Pay for Work of Comparable Worth: the Experience of Industrialised Countries*, Labour Market and Social Policy: Occasional Papers, No. 6, Paris: OECD.

Plantenga, J. and Velzen, S. van (1993) *Wage Determination and Sex Segregation in Employment; the Case of the Netherlands*, External report commissioned by and presented to the European Commission, Utrecht: Economic Institute/CIAV.

Remick, H. (ed.) (1984) *Comparable Worth and Wage Discrimination*, Philadelphia: Temple University Press.

Rubery, J. (1991) *Equal Pay and Institutional Systems of Pay Determination*, Equal Opportunities Unit – DG V, Brussels: Commission of the European Communities.

—— (1992) 'Pay, gender and the social dimension of Europe', Paper for the Seminar 'Job Evaluation: an Equal Value Perspective', Oxford: 2–4 July.

Social Europe (1991) *Equal Opportunities for Women and Men*, 3/91, DG V, Luxembourg: Office for Official Publications of the European Communities.

Sorensen, E. (1987) 'Effect of comparable worth policies on earnings', *Industrial Relations; A Journal of Economy and Society*, 26(3), pp. 227–39.

Stigt, J. van (1994) *Een Verkennend Onderzoek naar de Mogelijkheden en Problemen van de Introductie van Comparable Worth: een Concreet Voorbeeld*, OR 03–ER IV/1994, Den Haag: Emancipatieraad.

Treiman, D.J. and Hartmann, H.I. (1981) *Women, Work and Wages; Equal Pay for Jobs of Equal Value*, Washington DC: National Academy Press.

Veldman, A.G. and Wittink, R. (1990) *De Kans van Slagen; Invloeden van Culturen en Regels op de Loopbanen van Vrouwen*, Leiden: Stenfert Kroese.

INDEX